DISCOVERING THE HILL TOWNS OF
ITALY

DISCOVERING THE HILL TOWNS OF
ITALY

PAUL DUNCAN

PHOTOGRAPHS BY

JOHN FERRO SIMS

Clarkson Potter, Publishers
New York

For Aileen Low

Text copyright © 1990 by Paul Duncan
Photographs copyright © 1990 by John Ferro Sims
Photographs on pages 75, 76, 77 copyright © Ghigo Roli 1990

Designed by Andrew Barron & Collis Clements Associates

Published by Clarkson N. Potter, Inc.,
201 East 50th Street, New York, New York 10022

Published in Great Britain by Pavilion Books Limited in 1990

CLARKSON N. POTTER, POTTER and colophon
are trademarks of Clarkson N. Potter, Inc.

Manufactured in Spain

Library of Congress Cataloging-in-Publication Data
Duncan, Paul.
Discovering the hill towns of Italy / by Paul Duncan.
p. cm.
ISBN 0-517-57449-7: $22.95
1. Italy—Description and travel—1975– 2. Mountain life—Italy.
3. Cities and towns—Italy. I. Title.
DG430.2.D86 1990
945—dc20
89–8616
CIP

CONTENTS

INTRODUCTION

It would be possible to write volumes about the hill towns of Italy, if only because there are so many of them. Most Italian towns, if they aren't in the flat bits of Emilia Romagna, Lombardy or the Veneto, are built on some kind of incline. Samuel Butler, writing at the end of the nineteenth century, said that 'Italians seem hardly able to look at a high place without longing to put something on top of it.' He surmised that this was a remnant of some subliminal instinct much the same as that which 'makes sheep like to camp at the top of a hill; it gives a remote sense of security and vantage against an enemy'.

I have chosen to look at a mixture of lesser known hill towns as well as some of the old favourites. My preferences in either case have been governed by a quest to discover something truly original, something so bizarre as to be astonishing, or simply to give a lesser known but interesting place a chance to explain itself and therefore court popularity. Traipsing into remote mountain eyries I was inevitably stared at, watched and scrutinized, or else jeered at by adolescents mindful that my hobnailed boots and tartan trousers were not your average *paesan* wear. I was even chased away by an old rustic in semi-medieval dress when I nearly drove over her duck.

Routes have been suggested and distances between the various places noted, though this is not a travel guide in the conventional sense. It isn't bossy and insistent, because it isn't my intention to aid the visitor, nannylike, with snippets of train timetables and lists of alternative routes. There are no opening times of museums and closing times of parish churches, which in Italy can easily change from day to day anyway. There are plenty of travel guides that do all of that; gazetteer style, they gather you up and whisk you through the peninsula with hardly time to catch breath.

Instead, *Discovering the Hill Towns* is a slow easy look at Italy that gives you time to stop and sample local food and wine, to sit in the sun in the *piazze* with the old men in their grey hats, and to look at one or two monuments. If you don't want to visit every hill town in Italy, see every work of art, or rush to every festival, don't worry. Just see a few of each, but don't, like Henry James, attempt the rest after lunchtime's second bottle of dry red: his tipsiness cost him several interesting views. And don't hurry from one to the other in the rain and at top speed, as I did on a weirdly serpentine Umbrian country road. I ended up crumpled, with my car in a heap, at the bottom of an embankment. Two farmhands hauled me out and away to the farm-

Pitigliano in Tuscany (previous page) *seems to be falling off the edge of its rock. In Apulia* (above), *the houses are punctuated by sculptured portals.* (Left) *A typical hilltown silhouette.*

stead, where they fortified my flagging spirits with quantities of a home-produced brew, the local *vino santo*.

This book provides you with an idea of where to go and what to expect to see when you get there. Each chapter mentions a range of hill towns and small villages that have strange festivals, where the rituals might be part pagan part Christian, and characteristic local dishes which are either repellent or utterly delicious, according to individual taste. Bizarre local historical events are included, as are their main protagonists. Early travellers' findings in a particular region are mentioned where possible as a measure of the area's interest nowadays, and there are references to some local artists, architects and writers, and to current daily life.

The variety of local character, and colour, even within a small district, is astonishing. This is because, until the Risorgimento, Italy was a multiplicity of different states, some of which were no bigger than a single town and the countryside surrounding it. Whatever its size, each had its own social structure and way of life. Although Italy is a single state now, regionalism survives and, particularly in the south, is perpetuated by the high mountainous landscape and inaccessible valleys. Old traditions, customs and lifestyles that in any other country would have long since faded away persevere and are revered here very much as they always have been. Consequently southern Italy is fascinating, and because travellers, foreign as well as Italian, prefer the better known pleasures of Tuscany or the Veneto, it has been my intention to point out what they are missing by avoiding the foot of Italy's boot.

The more obvious cases of this preservation of old ways are found in Calabria, Basilicata, the Abruzzo, Sicily and Sardinia, regions that are far poorer than the more developed northern and central parts of Italy. In Central Italy there is a self-conscious desire to preserve local character – the festivals, cooking, architecture

The church of the Madonna della Rupestre, Castelmezzano in Basilicata.

and crafts individual to a particular area. In an effort to hang on to old cultural traditions, the *comune* (town council) in places like Tuscany, which is home to a great variety of foreigners and Italians from other regions as well as Tuscan Italians, inevitably package their annual events neatly to attract passing tourists. The origins of a religious ceremony, or a festival dealing with the fertility of the land for example, so obvious not fifty years ago to all those who took part, are obscured now that the 'locals' are often outsiders. Furthermore, the individual characteristics of one community are becoming increasingly indistinguishable from those of another. In some places these traditional celebrations have been turned into theatre, even pantomime, with elaborate costumes and often irrelevant peripheral events, which have been designed to provide income for the community.

In the sparsely inhabited and inaccessible parts of Calabria and Basilicata there are still communities where antique costume is worn as part of everyday life. In some places the people still speak with traces of ancient Greek in their dialects. In others life is almost medieval, and the values of the inhabitants have more in common with those of their ancestors of a hundred years ago than with, for example, most Italian city-dwellers today. These are closed, insular places where outsiders are stared at with incredulity.

But perhaps the strangest places in the south, most of them in Calabria, are those where antique Albanian is the mother tongue. Some of these communities are as insular as they were when they were first settled in the fifteenth century, when refugees poured into southern Italy from Albania. Shop and street signs are bilingual, and the bars are often full of confusion for travellers: old rustics try to assert

The carved balluster of a staircase in Pescocostanzo, Abbruzzo (left) *contrasts with the church of San Michele dei Greci* (right) *which juts out at the end of the town of Rivello, Basilicata.*

themselves by speaking to you in some obscure Calabrese dialect, or worse still, old Albanian, while the bar lady offers little help in strangely accentuated modern Italian. In these areas sign language, nods and smiles are the best methods of communication, especially if they insist on plying you with their local brew, so red that it looks like blood. Its alcoholic strength generally matches the density of its hue, and communication in any verbal manner is irrelevant after a couple of glasses of it.

Very often the old southerners speak nothing but dialect. Often the inhabitants of remote country villages are descended from clans of bandits who, by tradition, never came into contact with ordinary Italian because their families were always in hiding in the mountains. Generally, though, these verbose old rustics were shepherds, and a lifetime spent solitarily tending the flock on some lonely peak month

after month didn't provide much opportunity for broader linguistic or even conversational exchange.

The town of Cocullo in the Abruzzo has a strange festival which is inextricably bound up with the land, religion and the locality's pagan past. It is basically pagan, with a Christian overlay, and snakes and the local saint are the main protagonists; the snakes were once the sacrificial victims of the event, and the saint was the local deity, who took the place of the original pagan goddess and gave respectability to the festival in the eyes of the church. The deity, San Domenico Abate, has been accredited with the power to protect the population against, among other things, snakebite, and a procession where the statue of the saint is draped in writhing snakes is the high point of the event. It is enacted each year with an intensity which indicates both a strong belief in the power of ritual and an

The churches of Ostuni, Apulia, are the only buildings which aren't whitewashed.

intense fear of snakebite, in a region where most of the male population still work on the land as shepherds. This kind of festival is part of the life of the people, as important to them as the changing of the seasons.

This event doesn't have the sparkle and the sense of pageantry of festivals in, say, Tuscany or Umbria. At Cocullo the people appear in their worn country suits and their old cardigans; only the saint is brightly painted, and festive costumes, if they are brought out, are limited to antique functional aprons over long dark skirts. Here the faces of the people are drawn, set with an intensity which wills San Domenico to answer their prayers. Beads of sweat line the foreheads and the upper lips of the women as they reach out, straining to touch a snake. If they do, they believe they will acquire greater fertility, longevity and protection against illness.

In the south, sellers of love potions and amulets are not uncommon, and on the façades of some of the houses, particularly in Sicily and Basilicata, it is not unusual to find devices against the evil eye gouged out of the wall. This is also the part of Italy where you might find a statue of the Madonna smashed in a ditch next to her shrine; someone has blamed her for failing to intercede in some private matter. Equally, if she has 'interceded', and the donkey did last another winter, then the Madonna is rewarded. Not that this doesn't happen in Liguria or Umbria, but in the south these actions have a greater intensity and are much more in evidence.

It would take years to examine the minutiae of life in somewhere like Basilicata. Here, cut off from the rest of the world, and remarkably under-visited, the remains of the culture and the superstitions of old Europe are still flourishing. And you could fill books about the area, analyzing the reasons, other than the rough inhospitable landscape, for which these old ways continue. A visit to Basilicata is recommended above every other region in this book.

Instead of the more usual north to south approach, *Discovering the Hill Towns of Italy* begins with Sicily and ends with Piedmont in the north, and it gives preferential treatment to the south as a way of illuminating the lesser known regions. For many travellers to the peninsula, there is still no Italy beyond Rome.

The less interesting (to me) parts of the country have been given less space while the regions of Lombardy, Emilia Romagna, Val d'Aosta Trentino-Alto Adige, Friuli Venezia-Giulia, Campania and Molise have been omitted completely. The more interesting towns of Emilia are on the plain and all the other regions had the scales tipped against them in favour of their neighbours. Whichever part of the country you choose to visit, it is essential first to check the dates of local festivals and events with the Italian State Tourist Office. These are sometimes subject to change without reason, wherever you may be going. Likewise, restaurants and hotels come and go, and a rough prearranged schedule of where you might stay en route through the hill towns of the Italian countryside, particularly in Tuscany and Umbria, would be a good idea.

Serralunga d'Alba in Piedmont's morning mist (left). *The impregnable upper town of Bomarzo (above) in Lazio is now peppered with windows and openings. From afar it is indistinguishable from the rock on which it stands.*

SICILY

ENNA · CALASCIBETTA · LEONFORTE · NICOSIA
MISTRETTA · PIAZZA ARMERINA · CALTAGIRONE

Sicilians probably have less Italian blood in their veins than any other Italian national. Biologically and culturally they are an odd distillation of all those who have come to Sicily since the beginning of recorded history: Greeks, Carthaginians, Romans, Vandals, Ostrogoths, Byzantines, Saracens, Normans, Swabians, Angevins, Aragonese, Catalans, Neapolitan Bourbons, Piedmontese, French and English. Sicily was a free-for-all tramping ground and a victim of its location. Because of its situation on an east–west route through the Mediterranean Sea, the island quickly became a crossroads and a battlefield for growing Mediterranean civilizations.

Many of the hill towns of Sicily are a microcosm of the island's early history. As conquerors came and went, they left behind a deposit of cultural material ranging from customs and language to art and architecture. All this the islanders gradually assimilated and then reproduced in a uniquely Sicilian form. The resulting eclecticism is what is most characteristic of the Sicilian vernacular in virtually every field. Conversely, hundreds of years

of rule by foreigners brought with it oppression that bred insularity, resentment and poverty. Most of all, the comparative failure of post-war regeneration has driven people to call Sicily backward. But the problem is really one of stagnating local politics, of a system caught in a web of Mafia intrigue, as well as the continuing exclusion of the island from the Italian political mainstream. This obscures the reality of Sicily, an island anything but eternally backward. Sicily's problem is simply one of a decline from greatness.

Enna was once the most important town in the interior of the island. One of the most ancient hill towns in Sicily, it was coveted for its lofty strategic position practically in the centre of the island, and for the fertile wheat fields, olive groves and orchards which surround it. Evidence of its material wealth throughout its history – coins, bronzes, jewellery and military equipment – can be seen in the Treasury of the Duomo and the Museo Alessi in the Via Roma.

Today Enna is the provincial capital and, surrounding it on the valley floors, the bleached stubble of the wheat fields after the harvest still

Precipitous streets and stairways (above) *make shopping an arduous daily event. Most people have scooters, the noisy, polluting bane of Italian urban life. Eleanora, wife of Frederick II of Aragon* (right), *began the Duomo in Enna which was restored much later by the Spaniards.*

17

indicates a certain prosperity. Enna is lucky. The hedgerows between its fields are enriched with wild flowers and grassy banks. Yet thirty or forty miles to the east the landscape is desolate, the earth powdery and useless. Where cacti haven't colonized a rocky outcrop there might be a hill village, remote, possibly even deserted. Nothing moves out here. The sun is relentlessly hot and visions of Africa are never too far away from the mind.

Enna is in the 'navel of Sicily'. It was the centre of the cult of Demeter, the Greek goddess of fertility, who fulfilled her role so prodigiously that Sicily became a sort of Garden of Eden to the ancients. The Rocca di Cerere (Cerere was the Roman version of Demeter) at the eastern extremity of the town is the site of her temple, and according to Cicero there was a giant statue of her here, poised above an enormous drop to the valley below. Enna has a strange relationship with ancient mythology. The town and its surrounding landscape are part of a twilight world where legend and history meet. From the Rocca, or fortress, you can see the site of the abduction by Hades of Demeter's daughter Persephone. Persephone was picking roses and violets on the shores of Lago di Pergusa, to the south-east of the Rocca, when the Lord of the Underworld emerged from a nearby cave and carried her off on a golden chariot. On discovering the absence of her daughter, whose shrill cries, according to Homer, were ignored by both mortals and immortals, Demeter went into a miserable decline that prevented the corn in Sicily from growing. A famine threatened to engulf the island. Zeus took pity on her and decided that Persephone should spend half the year as Queen of the Underworld and the other half as a dutiful daughter. He duly allowed her to emerge from the underworld, and she then went on to become one of the presiding female deities of Sicily.

The people of Enna are very conscious of these deities, particularly of Persephone, whose memory is recorded in the Via Persephone, and you can still pick wild violets and irises near Hades's cave. What's more, in Piazza Francesco Crispi, at the centre of Enna, there is a much revered representation of her abduction by Hades, a copy in bronze of Bernini's original now in the Villa Borghese in Rome.

Demeter is supposed to have been buried deep within the Castello di Lombardia just below the Rocca. But this Castello is so massive that it could conceal a multitude of secrets, any one of which could easily have given rise to such a myth. It was built by Frederick II Hohenstaufen, and originally it had twenty towers. Only seven now remain. To get to it I had to cross the wide junction at the top end of the Via Roma and the Viale Paolo e Caterina Savoca, a fairground with bumper cars, avoiding crazed Sicilian females in disco gear, each one sucking a Madonna lollipop (in the form of the pop star not the Virgin) and each one thumping her thighs in time to the loud music. This is a far cry from the medieval armies that once camped here and within the castle itself. The only armies here nowadays are the youths who, on one occasion, assumed I was a German and crossed the piazza in my direction, to chat me up, I thought. I was disappointed to discover that all they wanted was to practise the Teutonic versions of 'yes please' and 'no thank you'. That was all.

Enna is a typical example of a Sicilian hill town, where the layers of history jostle with each other in competition for prominence. To isolate any one would be a pointless exercise. Although the town is mostly representative of the island's medieval past, of the destructive period between the extinction of Norman rule and the age when Sicily became a Spanish dependency, single buildings are piled with the accretions of all periods. Street patterns, if they weren't following the dictates of hill contours, followed whatever fashion was prevalent at the time. The Via Roma for example, the main artery of the town, is narrow and medieval in its upper reaches and, as it drifts downwards, winding along the contours of the hill towards the Piazza Vittorio Emanuele, becomes wider, more formal and the layout more nineteenth century. The *passeggiata* takes place in these lower reaches, where the potential for observing other people is unobstructed by odd medieval angles and strange twists between the buildings. In fact the lower reaches of the Via Roma are a seething mass of people from 5.30 p.m., when the roller shutters over shop windows are lifted and the drowsy veil of the afternoon siesta is pushed aside, until the middle of the evening. This is also the best time to walk up to the top of the Via Roma unhindered by strollers, past the Duomo and an assortment of strange baroque churches. The road is practically silent up here, and most of the churches can be visited each day until about 8.00 p.m.

The Duomo is a strange dumping-ground of styles, part fourteenth-century and part baroque, with gothic touches and a mostly six-teenth-century interior. It is a wonderful exam-ple of a building ravaged by the vicissitudes of Sicilian history. It was begun by Eleonora, the wife of Frederick II of Aragon, then restored and partially rebuilt by the Spaniards. Close inspection within reveals bits of classical carv-ing, probably from the Temple of Demeter, on the base of the stoup in a chapel in the north aisle. Another chapel on the left of the main altar sports one of the wilder essays of eighteenth-century Sicilian plasterwork stuck onto its gothic rib vaulting. Voluptuously fecund undergrowth – fruit, vegetables and flowers in plaster – tumbles from the ceiling, recalling Demeter's role, subconsciously transferred into the realms of the Church.

Sixteenth-century choir stalls, painted, gilded and now faded (possibly the work of Filippo Paladini), wobble above the nave beneath a tremendous wooden ceiling sup-

ported on Harpies, whose naked breasts are squeezed against the tops of the windows. Beyond a baldacchino nailed to a gilded cart, a side chapel has been converted for use by a local group discussing 'Drugs and their effect on Society'. (This quick switch to reality is a vital ingredient of Sicilian life in towns where it is easy to be swamped by the clutter of the past.)

The visual eclecticism displayed inside the Duomo is matched by a varied array of building styles lining the Via Roma itself. At number 467 an early baroque portal frames the entrance to the Palazzo Pollicarini, a fourteenth-century palace whose courtyard is ornately Arabic-Catalan in style; even more ornately, even decoratively, it is hung with sheets and pillow-cases drying in the sun. A bar, with a few old metal tables and seats, pokes out from beneath an antique archway in the courtyard, covered in vines, and a goat completes the scene. In Piazza Pietro Coppola, next to the Via Roma, is the Arabic-domed tower of the baroque church of San Francesco. Further on still, between Piazza Pietro Coppola and Piazza Vittorio Emanuele, is Piazza Garibaldi, a triumph of Italian Fascist architecture. An inscription on a pinnacle of the Palazzo del Governo proclaims Vittorio Eman-uele III '... Re d'Italia, Etiopia e Albania', while

Circuses and fairgrounds are common annual events at Enna, the centre of Sicily, and ones to which the inhabitants of all the nearby towns tend to gravitate.

underneath, scratched out though still partially legible, it goes on to laud Benito Mussolini '… Duce del Fascismo, Fondatore dell'Impero [and a date now obscured]'.

In the Piazza Francesco Crispi, facing the *Rape of Persephone*, is the Hotel Belvedere, an Art Deco fantasy of stained glass, mosaic and thin wooden veneers. Most of the bedrooms have 1920s furnishings and, since the hotel is poised over a precipice, over 300 metres above the bottom of the valley, most of the bedrooms also have incredible views. On a good day these extend as far as Mount Etna. Not for nothing is the Piazza also known as Piazza Belvedere. Daily the old men of the town, some in hats, some with their jackets over their shoulders, loll about against the wall of the piazza, admiring the view in much the same manner as guards in the past did, except that the guards would have been on the look-out for invading armies.

The Ristorante Belvedere is also in this piazza. Another restaurant, a better one in fact, where the food reflects nearly two thousand years of foreign occupation, is the Grotta Azzurra, in a tiny passageway off the Via Colajanni. The style of the cooking here is generally *cucina povera* – lots of stuffed vegetables and very yellow pasta accompanied by anything from sardines, pine nuts and raisins (*pasta con le sarde*) to hot peppers and tomatoes (*pasta all'arrabiata*). There is also *maccaruni di casa*, a very rough pasta dressed with a pork and tomato *ragù* and, very common in Sicilian restaurants, *pasta alla Norma*, named after Bellini's opera. It is worth noting that pasta first arrived in Sicily with the Arabs, only later spreading northwards. The local pasta is best followed by the local cheese called *piacentinu* which contains saffron and pepper.

Enna is on the main railway network of central Sicily. This doesn't add up to much, but it has its own railway station. It is a convenient main centre from which to visit other towns in the interior, most of which, because of the lie of

The countryside around Enna (right) *once provided the Roman Empire with all its grain requirements.* (Overleaf) *Piazza Armerina.*

the land, have no train links. Visitors have to use the bus.

The closest hill town to Enna is Calascibetta. You can see it from the windows of the Hotel Belvedere. Access is easy by bus or taxi because it is only a few miles away. Beyond it is Leonforte, with its own station, and beyond that, small, ancient Agira, dominated by its Saracen castle. Further on still are Nicosia and the Norman stronghold of Troina, both of which can only be reached by bus or car. All of these you can see by night from Enna, when their lights are on. During the day they tend to be obscured by the heat haze.

A deep valley separates Enna's black hulk from Calascibetta, dramatically situated on a rock opposite. Fortified by the Norman Count Roger in an attempt to take Enna in 1087, Calascibetta's dramatic aspirations, now supported only by its height and near impregnability, are diminished by a hopeless forlornness. Most of its churches are closed, and the central piazza is weighed down daily by unemployed youths shuffling about under the palms in the sun. When it gets too hot they gravitate towards the cafe, to sit out the afternoon heat in the cool shadows near the jukebox and the pool table.

The ramshackle houses of Calascibetta, mostly Saracenic in style and painted a deep reddish colour, struggle to keep standing. Surrounding them, a tangle of narrow streets at different levels is labyrinthine in its efforts to make you lose your way. The church and its adjoining convent at the top of the town gave up the fight to cling on, and a landslide tipped them over the edge of the precipice into the wheat fields below. Santa Maria del Carmelo, in the main piazza, threatens to do likewise unless repair work is carried out immediately. Inside, in the nave, a pathetic handwritten notice appeals for funds with which to restore a crumbling stucco façade covered with saints and a huge stucco sculpture of the *Visitation*. The odd 50,000 lire (about £24) has been given by anxious citizens,

but after an appeal lasting a year, a total of 650,000 lire (about £320) isn't very much for a façade thirty-five metres high. But Sicilians are fatalistic people. If the church collapses, well, there is always another.

This depressing spectacle is not unique in Sicily, though it is unmatched in the vicinity of Enna. Leonforte, about fifteen kilometres across the wheat fields to the north-east of Calascibetta, is much more uplifting. Its buildings, the colour of pale clay, seem to grow from the rich cornfields that surround it. Unusually, in a region where the hill towns are generally subject to the whims of the landscape, the centre of Leonforte has a great sense of urban dignity. As in a great capital, but on a miniature scale, the main street, Corso Umberto, slopes gently in a straight line, down through the circular Piazza Margherita to the Palazzo Branciforte at its lowest point. Crossing the piazza, and at right angles to the Corso, is a vista that terminates in two straight staircases, beyond which you can see the wilder, and more usual, passages and steep alleys typical of any hill town.

Evidence of Caltagirone's ceramic industry.

Leonforte was once the centre of a fiefdom which belonged to the princes of Branciforte, one of the richest and most powerful families in Sicily. Like all Sicilian landowners, they had feudal lordship over their estates, but unlike most, who rarely visited the country, the Branciforte were frequent visitors. Their palace is now partially disused, but it is still connected visually to the Granfonte, a huge fountain at the bottom of the southern slope of the town. This remarkable construction was built in 1651 by one of the Branciforte princes. Twenty-four jets spurt water into a stone trough beneath an elaborate architectural screen, a strange creation whose extremities are an even stranger rendering in stone of an oriental carpet, partially unravelled. Although the houses of Leonforte are all connected to the municipal water supply, *contadini* (farmworkers) on donkeys still stop at the Granfonte on the way to their fields, to fill terracotta amphorae or plastic bottles, which are then slung over the animal's back. Local women still wash their laundry on stone slabs in front of the water trough, which is something of a local meeting place on the road that wanders around the base of the town. Children kick their footballs against the fountain and chickens scratch the damp ground in its shadows.

Near the Granfonte is another Branciforte fountain, in the form of a grotto. Here water once sprang from a lion's head set into chunks of tufa, and was then transported into a huge basin below, lined with blue and white tiles. It is worth remembering that the Sicilian aristocracy were not noted for their acts of benevolence towards their feudal dependants; as seventeenth-century civic conveniences, the Granfonte and the grotto are most unusual.

Leonforte has an air of confident prosperity about it. But Nicosia, about twenty kilometres beyond it, has been ravaged by so many earthquakes that nearly all the streets have suffered some kind of rupture, and interesting early buildings are on the point of collapse. An important medieval centre, Nicosia was shaken by a landslide in 1757 and an earthquake in 1968, and was ravaged by a flood in 1972. Like Enna, it is full of buildings from all periods and, even in their decrepitude, most are worth visiting. On one side of the Piazza Garibaldi, at the centre of the town, are the headquarters of the Christian Democratic Party, split ominously down the middle by a huge crack. Next door, the Bar Roma is partially obscured by scaffolding, while the Duomo opposite is shored up by huge wooden plates in an effort to catch falling angels, stone fruit and birds as they dislodge themselves from the walls and the roof. This lovely old wreck, called San Niccolò, has a fourteenth-century façade and campanile and a magnificent sculpted gothic portal, into which have been set superficial baroque baubles and twists. On the north side of the building, facing Piazza Garibaldi, is a fourteenth-century arcade, one extremity of which has been converted into the Bar Centrale.

From the Duomo to Santa Maria Maggiore (founded in 1267), at the town's highest point, the Via Francesco Salomone wanders past small honey-coloured palaces, richly decorated with stone-carved potbellied herms, Titans and gargoyles, and linear architectural decoration.

Caltagirone is an important centre for ceramics; it always has been and any available piece of wall or ground surface is plastered with decorative ceramic tiles.

Number 37–39 is a good example, and is lavishly enriched without any sense of theoretical accuracy. This naïve quality, while provincial, is the most charming aspect of some of the buildings of Sicily.

Apart from the Duomo, the most important church in Nicosia is Santa Maria Maggiore. The façade of this huge building is covered with baroque twirls, which are mixed in with Greek acanthus patterns and stone fretwork relief.

This uniquely Sicilian fantasy was added to the thirteenth-century structure after the landslide of 1757. The campanile collapsed in the most recent earthquake, and, although its bells have been strung up on a beam between two makeshift posts to one side of the building, the Sunday chimes are now electronically transmitted. Electric lights have been wrapped around the stone fronds and tendrils of the entrance portal, and beyond their festive flashes is the

The polychrome mosaics of the Villa Imperiale probably date from about the fourth century AD.

statue of San Michele, one of Antonello Gagini's most impressive works. All around the church, and the massive pointed boulders of the rock on which it stands, are little cultivated plots full of spinach and tomatoes. Wire trellises have colonized parts of the pavement, and chickens have been cooped in pens in narrow spaces between the buildings.

This type of urban arcadia is more prevalent where the streets have been roughened by earthquakes, and the rubble of fallen buildings still remains to be cleared away. At the bottom of the Via Diego Ansaldo, where a convent lies toppled in a heap among the fig trees, bits of decorated tile and beautifully cut stone jut out of banks of wild red poppies, and cats stalk green lizards around the bases of old window seats and shutters. These wild gardens have none of Piazza Garibaldi's desolation on hot summer afternoons. There, on the stinging hot

You can see Calabiscibetta from the windows of the Hotel Belvedere at Enna, glowering at the latter from across the valley.

cobbles, the cicadas can only manage a listless and intermittent rattle. Nothing else stirs. Old men have dragged their chairs into the shade along the front wall of the Palazzo Pretorio, where they remain inert in a row. Their chins rest on their walking sticks or their heads are thrown back, their mouths open. Concentration on any worldly matter is long lost. Others have gone to the Circolo Ricreativo Fra Lavoratori in Via Francesco Salomone, a sort of working men's club, where they sit drowsily in groups playing cards at green baize tables. Others just sit sucking the smoke-filled air into their old sunken cheeks.

These old veterans are a fixture of most southern Italian towns. At Mistretta, in the Nebrodi hills, between Nicosia and the sea, they are an institution. Via Libertà, the main street bridging the town's two highest points, has three clubs for their entertainment. There is a workers' union, a working men's club, and a club for war veterans. The latter is fitted out like a gentleman's club in London, with red leather-covered benches lining the walls and a large centrally placed table piled with newspapers. These, on closer inspection, turn out to be mostly the same edition of the *Corriere dello Sport*. Old rustics sit here in their droves, picking their teeth, doing nothing, reading, dozing; on Sundays they are always sober in dark suits and uncomfortable in ties. All the clubs face each other across the triangular junction of the Via Libertà and the Piazza Guglielmo Marconi, and craggy ancients potter in and out from one to the other.

Mistretta comes alive on Sundays, when the town is flooded with locals on their day off. Mixing in with them are villagers from the surrounding hills, who have come in to amuse themselves: for them Mistretta is an important centre of diversion. Not much happens here during the week, when most people are out working in the shops on the coast or in the ceramic factories of Santo Stefano Camastra

sixteen kilometres away. Others drive out to work in the fields – few people actually live in the countryside – only coming back for lunch or at the end of the day. But if it is a Sunday or a religious feast day, or the day of the spring First Holy Communions in the Chiesa Madre, Mistretta is packed. The shops are open, the Via Libertà is crowded all morning with strollers, and the Gran Bar is ransacked for espresso.

First Holy Communion day is practically a national day of celebration in Italy. In Mistretta, plastic red and white flags are flung across the Via Libertà and the principal alleyways and staircases off it, and a brass band marches around the piazza heralding the arrival at Mass of the First Communicants. Small girls dressed as brides, demure in white nylon, are led self-consciously up the aisle by boys dressed rather ludicrously as a cross between choirboys and angels. Each carries a single white lily, which by the end of the service has been reduced to a wreck of petals and squashed stalk.

In order to watch the preliminaries, I squeezed into an empty spot beside some farmers leaning against an Alfa Romeo with a furry seat. There is no order in these celebrations. Every participant is driven by some inner impulse to behave in whatever manner suits him

Sculpted stemme, coat of arms (left), proclaims the importance of some now long defunct local family. (Above) Old men sit about listlessly just out of reach of the afternoon sun lazily gossiping, dozing, picking their teeth or doing nothing at all.

municants then rush out of the fifteenth-century entrance portal, beneath the gaze of a statue said to be by Giovanni da Milano, past the brass band sweating in the shadows of the Palazzo Pretorio, to the Giardino Pubblico at the top of the Via Roma, to play on the swings and tear their outfits among the cacti, the palms and the box hedges.

In the seventeenth century Mistretta was a fairly wealthy town. Some of its patrician glamour remains in the rich decorations adorning the palaces in the main street. The Gran Bar itself, in the Via Libertà, occupies what was the entrance to a substantial seventeenth-century house. The entrance canopy is made up of a pediment supported by vast potbellied herms, while the original internal staircases, one on either side of the bar, are now converted to hold a selection of chocolates and potted palms.

As the Via Libertà climbs the hill it becomes the Via Roma. At number 146 Via Roma there is an interesting old *farmacia*, whose walls are lined with cases in a Strawberry Hill gothic style, and further on are one or two interesting wooden nineteenth-century shop fronts. The town's churches, apart from the principal Chiesa Madre, are very difficult to gain entry to. San Sebastiano, with its baroque façade and Arabic-domed campanile, in the Via Libertà, is practically derelict, and the vast statue of the dying St Sebastian threatens to collapse into the street. There are two others – the Chiesa del Carmine and the Chiesa di San Francesco.

From the remains of the Castello di Mistretta, way above the town, you can see the sea and the Aeolian Islands to the north. The whole of the town is laid out below, on a saddle between the castle rock and the peaks of the hills beyond, with the block-like rust-coloured houses dropping gently in terraces down the slopes of the mountain. Beyond the outer perimeter of the town are fields, herds of goats, and one or two old abandoned Fiat 500s rusting in heaps.

or her best. Luck sometimes makes their impulses coincide, and this series of accidents calls itself an 'event'. My instinct, I decided, as I continued to lean against the Alfa, would have been to inject a little order into the occasion, sorting out those who were genuine participants from those who were just standing around. Even in the church, while the women are crammed at the front of the church, men of all generations wander in and out in a Byzantine fashion, chatting in groups or smoking. Even the service is a chaotic ritual that the priest doesn't seem to have any control over. His words are drowned by whispers and arguments between delinquent small 'brides', hellbent on anything but a saintly existence, and young male angels all in white. But I suppose all this adds to the free flow of life, and is an ingredient of the essential difference between northern Europeans and southerners.

After Mass each 'bride' struggles into a side chapel to have her picture taken beneath a brightly painted statue of the Virgin, whose outstretched arms and fingers are hung with hundreds of wedding rings, gold and silver bracelets and gold watches. The First Com-

Caltagirone, like Piazza Armerina, has a glut of Baroque buildings.

Mistretta makes no effort to project any particular image to tourists. It can be reached only by bus or private car; there is no railway connection (the nearest station is at Leonforte). There is a single tiny hotel and a couple of *trattorie* without names. One, hidden down a small alley behind the church of San Sebastiano, has a sign outside its door which simply announces '*Tavola Calda*', a notice of intent to produce food at recognized times throughout the day. The cooking provided is simple *cucina povera* washed down with home-produced *vino locale*, which, in places like this, will invariably be very individualistic and rich in flavour and scent.

South of Enna are Piazza Armerina and Caltagirone, two hill towns slightly bigger than those already mentioned. Piazza Armerina, accessible from the station at Caltagirone, is a very pleasant place, whose main attraction is the Imperial Roman villa at Casale, a short distance outside the town. A few pleasant hours can be spent wandering around Piazza's main lanes and alleyways. The amount of light that enters these deep arteries is restricted because the balconies that jut out over them are covered in potted plants and stacked with cages full of chickens and blackbirds. In Piazza Armerina each balcony is different: some have supports carved with grotesque faces of people or animals; some are stone, some cast or wrought iron; others are surrounded by wrought-iron sunflowers, whose petals double up as extremely nasty spikes intended to deter intruders.

The streets rising from the Piazza Garibaldi are most popular early in the evening. The usual procession of strollers following some imaginary line along the ground fills up the streets and, in order not to miss the fun, old women sit out on the balconies, using them much as one would use a private box in an opera house, and pass comments to one another across the street or down to some hapless passer-by. These 'boxes' are very useful during

Piazza's annual pageant, the Palio dei Normanni, which, rather perversely, celebrates Count Roger's taking of the town in the eleventh century for the Normans. There is a processional entry into the town on 13 August and, the next day, a ceremonial joust.

The lasting impression of Piazza Armerina is of a glut of baroque buildings. The same could be said of Caltagirone, about fifty kilometres to the south-east, straddling a deep ravine. Here the baroque churches and public buildings of the town's centre surpass themselves in sheer extravagance, creating the effect of a town composed entirely of stage-set architecture. Not only this, but everywhere you look there is evidence of Caltagirone's importance as a centre for ceramics. So prolific were the town's ceramicists in the past that whole walls in the town are covered in decorated tiles, ceramic flowers and other devices. Caltagirone's vast staircase, La Scala, with its 142 steps leading up to the church of Santa Maria del Monte, is lined with tiles depicting Sicilian heraldic devices and figures from its legends and history. These steps are illuminated annually on 23 July, the Festival of San Giacomo.

*L*a Scala, with its 142 steps, is lined with ceramic
decorations, some of which relate events from
Sicilian folklore.

CALABRIA

PENTEDÀTILLO · GERACE · STILO · SPEZZANO ALBANESE
SAN DEMETRIO CORONE

dward Lear, travelling through Calabria in 1847, found a land scarred by deep ravines, full 'of horror and magnificence without end …' . His watercolours and sketches of southern Italy immortalize the parts that appealed most to his overtly romantic disposition, like the rocky chaos of the Aspromonte mountain range that rises from the Ionian Sea at the foot of Italy, where the stony gulleys and gorges ripping open the landscape are the result of centuries of earthquake activity. The hill towns of the Ionian coastline – Pentedàtillo, Bova, Gerace and Stilo – which populate his paintings, are dwarfed by their menacing surroundings, and his people seem small and helpless in a landscape of such savagery.

In Lear's day the wild ranges of the Aspromonte were very sparsely populated. They still are, though they are a great deal safer now than they were. A common feature of the inaccessible valleys and forests, where communication was extremely difficult, were the bands of brigands, sometimes numbering as many as three hundred men, who roamed the countryside terrorizing villagers in the remoter

outposts of 'civilization' and employing guerrilla tactics in their dealings with any travellers mad enough to enter the interior. They kidnapped for ransom, and even practised cannibalism in order to survive. One infamous brigand in the eighteenth century, called Mammone, is said to have boasted of having personally killed 455 people, drinking their blood from a skull that hung from his belt.

Against this murky backdrop a few hardy travellers still came to Calabria. They came looking for that extra frisson of danger to which life in Calabria would expose them. They also wanted to see for themselves the feudal lifestyle of the peasants and landowners, and to learn about their superstitions. They wanted to experience the pagan quality of the peasants' relationship with the land which, they were told, had successfully managed to sidestep Christianity and had thus maintained a continuity with the very distant past.

English travellers in Calabria were few and far between compared with the rest of Italy. Nonetheless they came, some, like Henry Swinburne and The Hon. Keppel Craven, with

*An apse of the Duomo in Gerace (above). The builders of the Duomo plundered the ancient building
sites of Locrii for material for their own building (right).*

a small army to provide protection. Others came with their wives and children. These travellers generally stuck to the bigger towns where, if the surrounding territory was particularly anarchic, the forces of law and order could gain easy access if there was a crisis. Craufurd Tait Ramage, a Scotsman who went to Calabria in 1828, went about on a donkey with an umbrella for protection against the sun. His only complaint was that his umbrella was too heavy. Only Lear ventured into the interior of the Calabrian countryside, though even he went no more than ten or twelve kilometres inland.

Today it is much easier to travel through Calabria: its hill towns have become much more accessible, and it should also be said that the countryside is no longer dangerous. In 1950 a government foundation, the *Cassa per il Mezzogiorno*, assisted in the opening up of the interior, building new roads and organizing the cultivation of land that had become arid owing to years of deforestation and neglect. In Lear's day the Aspromonte and the Sila country in the north, between the city of Catanzaro and Calabria's northern borders, were virtually roadless, and only after a hair-raising trek through forests and scrub would you arrive at your destination.

One old track, now called the SS 110, leads from the hill town of Stilo, on the edge of the vast Bosco di Stilo, north of the Aspromonte, to the towns of the interior. At intervals along its route there are little iron crosses, which mark the spot at which lone travellers were either murdered by bandits or killed off by the cold. Someone still remembers some of these poor unfortunates today: resting against the rusting memorial crosses are candles, often alight, in small red glass jars.

Stilo is no longer very remote; indeed, access is easy if you have a car. By comparison, Pentedàtillo, at the southern end of the Aspromonte, is suffocated by its own insularity and obscurity. This small town is huddled in the palm of a huge hand-like rock about ten

Gerace sits on a rocky outcrop way above the dried up River Novito.

kilometres from the Ionian coastline, at the tip of Calabria. Its inhabitants rarely descend the track that leads away from it to the road that connects it to the sea. Lear loved to paint it. No doubt he was inspired in his romantic dallyings with the paintbrush not only by the fearsome countryside of great boulders and scraggy bushes that surround the town but also by the gothic horror story that was staged here in the seventeenth century, the main protagonists of which were two local noble families driven by violence and revenge. Baron Montebello, lord of a huddle of cottages four kilometres to the north of Pentedàtillo, wanted to marry the daughter of Marchese Pentedàtillo, although she was already betrothed to a Neapolitan nobleman. The day after the wedding celebrations the baron broke into the castle of Pentedàtillo, murdered nearly every member of the marchese's family and carried off his daughter. By all accounts she rather fancied the baron and was pleased to be abducted. However, she hadn't expected to have her entire family assassinated in the process. As it happened, she died of guilt a month later, locked in her lover's castle at Montebello. To make amends for his terrible behaviour, the baron then took in a nephew of the dead woman, who had survived the original massacre, and made him not only his page but heir to the joint Montebello-Pentedàtillo estates. The youth rewarded the baron for his belated act of kindness by taking him prisoner, blinding him, and walling him up in the chamber of the castle at Pentedàtillo where the old Marchese Pentedàtillo and his family had met their end. But that wasn't all. An earthquake then shook Pentedàtillo and Montebello and both castles collapsed, killing everyone.

Bits of the castle at Pentedàtillo survive (and in the past you were enthusiastically told by the locals that you could still see the Pentedàtillo family blood on an old surviving wall); there is also an interesting little church dedicated to SS Pietro e Paolo. An hour or so would be enough

to take in this little town, whose houses – some sunbaked brown, others whitewashed – have been squeezed in among the rocks, fitting into crevices and clinging to one another in an effort to prevent themselves from sliding down the gravelly slope.

Pentedàtillo is one of a group of settlements founded by the Byzantines on this stretch of the Ionic coast. Roccaforte del Greco, Roghudi and Bova Superiore are others. Roccaforte is a fairly typical hill town, its buildings forming a crown around the pinnacle of a conical hill. Roghudi is rather more singular. A thin line of buildings, two or three houses deep, creeps along the spine of a hill; to one side is the vast dried-up river bed of the River Amendolea – a wild torrent in winter – and to the other is a narrow, deep ravine darkened by the shadows of overhanging rocks.

These three towns are among the very last in southern Italy where the inhabitants still speak a form of Greek. Perhaps it is a Byzantine dialect, or perhaps the remains of something far earlier – ancient Dorian possibly? If you listen into a domestic conversation or eavesdrop in a shop, you may be experiencing the very last link with the twilight days of ancient Greece. Who knows? Until now the remoteness of these towns has been instrumental in preserving their dialect. But in the Sixties, when new roads were built and television was introduced into these hilltop communities, the world suddenly opened up and the young departed. The dialect which has been passed down orally from one generation to another is now in danger of extinction.

Another Byzantine community where they spoke Greek a long time ago was Gerace. It sits on a rocky outcrop way above the dried up River Novito, not far from the sea. The inhabitants of this hill town make a daily pilgrimage to the market in Locri, on the coast, the nearest town with a station, to sell whatever is reared within the confines of Gerace itself. You see people

wandering down the mountain on foot or in old painted carts pulled by donkeys. The drivers of these carts are generally transfixed by the road ahead, oblivious to the danger of a pile-up of motorized traffic behind them. People walk by with geese shoved into plastic bags, a long neck and head sticking out to one side, the bird unaware of its intended fate under the butcher's knife; others lead goats on a piece of string; yet others drive small vans piled with boxes of tiny tomatoes, garlic and peppers from the family plot.

Gerace was once one of the most important towns in Calabria. Its rock was annexed by Byzantine refugees from Locri Epizephyrii, an important colony of Magna Graecia, fleeing the Saracen raids in the tenth century. The small oratory of San Giovanello at Gerace in the Piazza Tre Chiese survives from this period; so do the tiny ancient houses crowding around the town's little semi-private courtyards full of lemon trees, vines and geraniums. The Normans annexed Gerace in the eleventh century and adorned the town with their own monuments; the most important survival is the Duomo, the biggest in Calabria. As usual it was built using material from ancient building sites, in this case the temples of Locri. Twenty huge

Little old palaces with mullioned windows jostle with more ancient façades, some Norman, others Baroque (above). *(Overleaf) Fiats and widows in black – the most common sight in the southern hill towns.*

columns in green, white and yellow marble and granite divide the nave and the aisles. Other smaller columns, with decorative capitals, support the vault of the crypt.

Wandering through the narrow lanes of Gerace, bounded by high pebble-dash walls covered in prickly pears and wild roses, you see occasional Byzantine cupolas or Norman mullioned windows in old palazzo courtyards, and eighteenth-century wrought-iron balconies and handrails more typical of Sicilian towns. In the Via dell'Addolorata there is a small stuccoed baroque church with a pale pink, blue and green domed ceiling and an air of faded, bedraggled beauty. In glass boxes around the walls are plaster martyred saints dying a gentle death, more gentle perhaps than their Sicilian counterparts, who tended to die slowly from hideous wounds and bloody lacerations. Behind the faded green panelled box pews, a little back stair set into the wall climbs up to an organ loft where there is an

old ivory keyboard dated 1850. All around are piles of other saints, plaster figures of Christ and wooden *putti* that withered into dust when I touched them. This charming little church hasn't been used in years. There aren't enough people to fill it because the population of Gerace is dwindling.

But for those who remain, daily life carries on in much the same way as it has done for centuries. Every morning, just after sunrise, while the shadows of the buildings still cover the paving stones, the Piazza Tribunale is splashed with buckets of water in an effort to keep the dust at bay. The paving stones of the piazza, in a direct line of fire from the sun, will boil at midday, so, while the sun is still low, women in black make their way to the Via Zalenco and the shops.

In this lane connecting the Piazza Tribunale with the Piazza del Tacco the shops are really cavernous openings in the wall, leading to

Washing hanging out to dry in Gerace.

general dealers in anything from kitchen knives to pyjamas. Cheek by jowl with scythes and boxes of nails are pasta dishes, wine jugs displaying ancient Greek decorative motifs – zigzags and key patterns – which have never gone out of fashion in Gerace, and the corkscrews without which a visit to Italy is incomplete. The quest for missing corkscrews was a daily occurrence for me, so frequently did I lose them – even though inebriation was not the cause of my forgetfulness.

Number 22 Via Zalenco is the *cantina* which sells local wine straight from the barrel. Here I sluiced my parched throat with a (small) flagon before staggering out to the Piazza del Tacco to join the old men leaning on the wall outside the barber's shop, each reading his own copy of the *Corriere dello Sport* – the national sporting daily – for the football results. Not being a football fan, I stuck to Norman Douglas's *Old Calabria*.

Life is very slow in Gerace. Most of the young have left, preferring to work in Catanzaro or Cosenza. They no longer care for a leisurely shave with a cut-throat razor at the barber's in the piazza, or want their clothes made by the tailor at number 13 Angolo di Via Roma già della Spezzeria. Thick jackets in thorn-proof tweed are not attractive to them, nor in fact very useful to would-be sophisticates with no interest in the rural life. So the tailor sits all day in his Fifties-style workshop, doing the mending and gazing out through the nearby Porta del Sole at the bottom of the street that slopes away from his door, and out to the sea in the distance.

The Ionic coast is cluttered with little towns like Gerace, the important ones no more than seven or eight kilometres inland. Continuing along the SS 106 from Gerace, past Locri, are Caulonia and Stilo, both very typical examples of Calabrian hill towns. Plotting a course on a map, it would seem at first that the best way to get to these highland places is along the inland passes; distances on the map seem minimal. But no Calabrian would ever dream of going that way, over the mountains. They would only ruin their gears, twisting and turning through the dizzy heights of the Calabrian peninsula. The road along the coastal plain is best, turning off it and going inland whenever you need to.

Stilo, a rough town clinging to the side of Monte Consolino, fifteen kilometres from Caulonia as the crow flies, has some very interesting buildings as well as the most important monument in Calabria. Above the town, on a rocky platform, is the Cattolica, a small chapel built by the Byzantines in about the ninth century. Its five flat-topped domes are supported by walls of delicately patterned brickwork; the interior measures only six metres by six metres, and is decorated with Byzantine frescoes from three different epochs. Four columns, which came from some nearby antique building, hold up the roof; the first of these, nearest the door, was placed upside down so that the capital is nearest the floor, signifying the defeat of paganism.

Holy Week celebrations at Stilo are a very long-drawn-out affair. Nearly all the locals take part. On Holy Thursday bare-footed 'penitents', both males and females of all ages, trudge through as many of the town's alleys and passages as they can, each carrying on their

The rough pebble-dash walls lining the labyrinthine passages and streets of Gerace are solid and shabby.

shoulders a large, heavy cross. On Good Friday they accompany a statue of Our Lady of Sorrows, the Madonna Addolorata, from the Chiesa Madre, a vast, partially Norman edifice, to San Giovanni Theresti, a baroque church on the edge of the town. Behind the statue the street throngs with men singing songs, the origin and meaning of which are part Christian and part pagan, a mixture that nobody really understands. In the very last procession, retracing the route from San Giovanni Theresti back to the Chiesa Madre, the penitents carry a large figure of the dead Christ wrapped up in a huge sheet.

On these occasions some of the penitents carry *gucciadate*, huge ring-shaped cakes, which are either impaled on long thin crosses made of cane or worn like huge bracelets. Everyone, throughout the week, eats *dolci*, sweets, which have been prepared according to traditional recipes. In fact, the festive *dolci* of Stilo are famous. There are the *pitte di San Marco*, a nutty mass mixed with dried figs, eggs and flour, the *'nzulle*, made from flour, sugar and ammonia, and, most popular at Easter, the *cuzzupe*, little cakes made from eggs, flour and milk and moulded into the shapes of baskets, fish and hearts. Visitors to Stilo on these occasions can eat at either the Trattoria La Cattolica or the Ristorante San Giorgio. Homemade pasta, aubergines stuffed with fresh tomato sauce and dusted with a pinch of *peperoncino rosso* (red chillies) and piquant salamis are the best things to eat here and they are all highly recommended by the locals.

In the north of Calabria, in the rugged countryside of the Sila Greca, is the town of Rossano. In contrast to the harsh, inhospitable terrain surrounding it, Rossano has one or two exquisite artistic gems that set it apart from any other town in Calabria. In the Museo Diocesano for example (in the Archbishop's Palace adjacent to the Duomo), is the Codex Purpureus, the sixth-century Rossano Gospels, said to be the oldest illustrated Gospel book in existance. The Greco-Byzantines of Calabria produced quantities of these; only one remains, incomplete – that of Rossano. Having distinguished itself on that score, Rossano also boasts one or two rather fine churches, in particular the twelfth-century church of the Panaglia and the tenth-century church of San Marco. This jewel-like edifice, resembling the little domed building at Stilo, stands at an extremity of the town, on a rocky cliff overlooking the gorge of the Celati torrent.

To the northeast, just before the Coscile River is swallowed up by the mountains of Basilicata, is the region often called 'Little Albania'. Insular and detached, this area offered protection to a variety of hilltop communities founded in the fifteenth century by Albanians fleeing their native country after the death of Skanderbeg, their leader against the Turks. Ten to fifteen years ago, towns like Spezzano Albanese and San Demetrio Corone were still closed against the outside world, cut off and inaccessible.

Norman Douglas was one of the few English travellers who bothered to visit this region; in fact, when he visited San Demetrio Corone earlier this century, he was told by the inhabitants that 'no Englishman has ever entered the town'. Nobody ever dared to come because of the danger of malaria from the nearby mosquito-infested plain, the Piana di Sibari, between the mountains and the sea. Douglas called these places 'islands of alien culture' where the people, having abandoned their homeland, its mountains, rivers, saints, costumes and ways of life, endeavoured to preserve whatever they could of their heritage in a foreign land. High in the mountains of Calabria that wasn't so difficult.

Spezzano Albanese is the largest of the Albanian hill towns. It could be called the capital of 'Little Albania'. Houses and churches drift along the crest of a flattish limestone hill;

Vespas – the scourge of the Italian hill towns.

there is nothing extraordinary about its appearance. It lies on the main road from Castrovillari to Cosenza, and its inhabitants drive Fiats, drink espresso and eat pasta like everyone else. But on closer inspection it is distinctly un-Italian. If Mediterranean geography were different and Italy and Albania shared a common border, this is what a frontier town would look like, superficially at least. The street signs are in a mixture of Albanian – the fifteenth-century version, called *Arbereschi* – and modern Italian. The inhabitants speak the dialect in the shops, barter in it at the market, and there is a local news sheet written in it.

The centre of activity at Spezzano Albanese is the Gran Caffè, in the town's main street. Its owner, an Albanian female with typically heavy, pronounced features, greets everyone who enters in the local dialect, her huge, gold, Balkan earrings jangling gypsy-style at every turn. There are variations of her all over this little town. In the *pasticceria*, in Via Albania, the baker's wife sits darning socks, wearing a long black dress partially covered with layers of starched lace aprons. A beautiful wide lace collar covers her shoulders, but she is anything but quaint in her old boots. Other, older, women in long dresses with tiny floral print patterns scuffle around the daily morning market, the Mercato Municipale, fishing about in sacks of beans and potatoes, or gossiping in the doorway of the communal laundry in the Via Albania, where mounds of washing are still scrubbed by hand in huge stone troughs. Thirty years ago there would have been goats in the streets, and chickens and pigs would have scratched about in the dust, feasting on whatever was flung from the open doorways.

On feast days, and especially at Easter, the inhabitants of the surrounding villages and towns flock to Spezzano Albanese. On these occasions the women generally wear their traditional costume; their town of origin is identifiable by its colour – bright orange or green,

electric blue or scarlet – and each part of the dress is worked with silver and gold thread. Again, thirty years ago these costumes would have been a common daily sight in every Albanian town.

Spezzano Albanese, a quiet pastoral town, erupts at Easter. Celebrations in one form or another begin on the Thursday before Easter Sunday and last until the Tuesday after. On Good Friday a procession leaves the church of the Madre di Gesù, goes down the Via Nazionale and enters the Church of the Carmine. Pilgrims are led by a line of the worthiest among them, who carry on their shoulders a coffin containing a statue of the body of the dead Christ. Immediately behind, some of the women bear a rather stricken-looking Virgin of Sorrows. Then come more women, in crudely tinted gowns with bright shawls over their heads, followed by the men. Heavy, dark, weather-beaten faces, reflecting some of the emotion of the event, strain under the weight of the loads. Funeral music alternates with the singing, in dialect, of songs of farewell to the dead. The occasion is dark and brooding. Christ and his mother have entered the realms of ordinary mortals, and the rhythmic scuffling on gravel of feet in procession, together with the music and the singing, not unlike eastern funeral wailing, creates a leaden atmosphere that is relieved later by drink.

The pinnacle of the Easter festivities is an event which takes place on the Sunday. Young girls from Spezzano decorate an ancient statue of the Virgin, kept in the Santuario della Madonna delle Grazie on the edge of the town, with gold jewellery and precious stones. As on Good Friday, the women follow tradition by dressing in Albanian costume, only this time they copy the Virgin and cover themselves in gold necklaces and brooches, and fix heavy bunches of gold charms to their ears. They wear veils embroidered with gold thread, and the jacket sleeves are covered in stars and flowers.

A car is essential in Little Albania. The country bus takes ages to get anywhere and, if your destination is San Demetrio Corone, frustratingly only a mere twenty kilometres from Spezzano Albanese as the crow flies, you should set aside at least two hours to get there. The road straggles down to the plain, skirts the Crati River and runs practically to ancient Sybaris on the coast before branching back on itself, between the rivers Mizofato and Muzzolito, and then winding back and forth, up and up to San Demetrio Corone on a fertile incline about nine hundred metres above sea level.

This idiosyncratic little place is completely Albanian. Whereas the purity of Spezzano Albanese has been poisoned by modern petrol stations and roadside advertisements, San Demetrio Corone continues to turn its back on the outside world and even on the olive and chestnut groves all around it. Its insularity is most singular, as if the inhabitants had more to preserve than other Albanian communities. It has the Italo-Albanian college, where priests are trained. Founded in 1792 by Ferdinand I, it once contained a celebrated library, and is still open to the public. The nucleus of the college is a little chapel dedicated to Sant'Adriano where, in the course of construction, the builders incorporated some antique columns and a tesselated pavement decorated with snakes, birds and leopards.

San Demetrio Corone also has, in pride of place, a statue of Skanderbeg on a pedestal in the little piazza at the top of the Corso Giorgio Castriotta o Skanderbek. Beyond, an unintelligible signpost points to places like Shën Sofia, Mbuzati and Maqi. Turkey? Albania? No, Calabria. Reassure yourself that this is Italy in the Bar Sport, in the Via Domenica Maura, an irregular cobbled lane between small houses admittedly more Greek-looking than Italian. Here a large poster of a Milanese football team looms over a row of dusty Cinzano bottles and a picture of Lake Como. The Bar Sport is really a

cantina. On hard wooden seats skirting the wall, old men sit in silence, their eyes glazed from too much of the local sweet port-like wine that the large Balkan blonde serves from beneath the counter. She chats to one customer in *Arbereschi* and to another in a Calabrese dialect. To me she speaks Italian.

Following the sign to Maqi (Macchia), the road clambers away from San Demetrio, up the mountainside, through the cypresses and wild bushes of bright yellow broom, to the Ristorante Bella Vista. It is run by a family who take it in turns to go up into the hills early in the morning to pick wild mushrooms and herbs for use in the cooking. They serve things like wild *porcini* (a variety of mushroom) with homemade pasta, and side dishes of *melanzane* (aubergines or eggplant), which are fried, or mashed and boiled, and then mixed with garlic and grated cheese, sliced in vinegar or stuffed with minced meat or anchovies and olives. There might be *rigatoni alla pastora* (pasta with ricotta, pecorino – a cheese made from sheep's milk – and bits of fried sausage) and there is always a handy half carafe of locally produced red or white wine, or a bottle of Ciro'Bianco or Rosso, ancient Greek in origin. The red Ciros of this area are always thick and velvety, capable of inducing long and very deep siestas.

The church of San Marco in Rossano.

BASILICATA

AND APULIA

RIVELLO · MELFI · CASTELMEZZANO
PIETRAPERTOSA · PISTICCI · SAN
GIOVANNI ROTONDO · OSTUNI

In the forests of Basilicata, wild boar and wolves are not uncommon. In the last century and earlier in this one, wolves were shot and killed with spring guns and dynamite or caught alive in steel traps; they still roam the countryside of the remoter parts of Basilicata today, and their numbers are sufficient to necessitate providing sheepdogs with ugly spiked collars with which to defend themselves from attack. Sheep grazing in the lonelier heights of Monte Pollino, straddling the Calabria–Basilicata border, or on Monte Vulture, an extinct volcano to the north, and among the dense oaks and chestnuts of the Sirino mountain range near Potenza, are their usual prey. Only rarely are shepherds and travellers selected for canine execution.

Everywhere else on the Italian peninsula wolves are a thing of the past. Only the remoteness and inaccessibility of the countryside, most of which is dramatically mountainous, has ensured their survival here. This factor has also proved the salvation of traditional ways of life in the hill towns of the region. The confined existence of cultural identities, customs and traditions is more marked here than in any other part of the Italian mainland.

Basilicata was once called Lucania, a name which it took from its earliest inhabitants, the Lucani. Under the Byzantines it was renamed Basilicata, from the Greek word *basilikos* which indicated its governor's standing as an administrator. Mussolini changed the name back to Lucania but it didn't stick, though the people of the region are still called Lucani. Basilicata has had as many outside influences as Calabria, and nearly as many as Sicily, and most of its towns have, or lie within easy reach of, Greek temples, Roman baths, Norman castles, medieval abbeys and great churches. But it has always been on the margins of the main communication routes and only on the periphery of historic events. It is a small region, one of the most sparsely populated in Italy.

All over Basilicata are little hill towns whose silhouettes are appealing from afar, each one built in the most inaccessible of places. The romance of the hill town is nowhere more

The twenty-two metre high statue of the Redeemer, made of Carrara marble, towers over Maratea (above). (Right) Maratea, seen from above, nestles beneath Monte San Biagio.

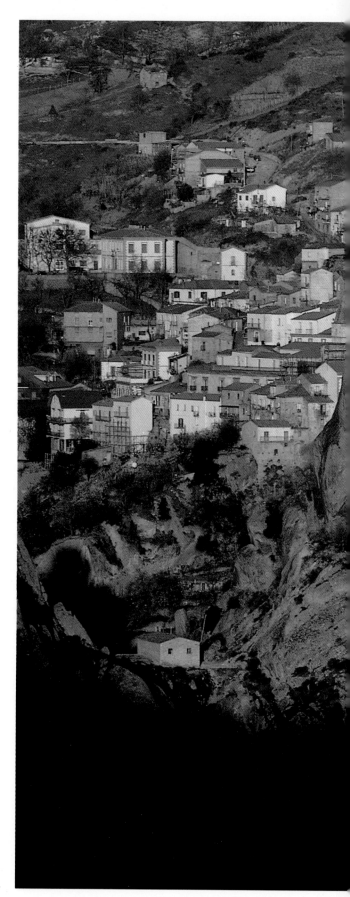

potent. Seen from below, they are like beacons of civilization in an alien and uncontrollable landscape. Carlo Levi, in his book *Christ stopped at Eboli*, describes the hill town in Basilicata to which he was banished for political reasons in the 1930s as 'a streak of white at the summit of a bare hill, a sort of imaginary Jerusalem in the solitude of the desert'.

Each town is a small community with perhaps two churches, a town hall and a single *trattoria*. Few have hotels and even fewer have connections with the railway. Travellers must rely on the blue country buses that run from either Potenza or Matera, the two provincial capitals. In western Basilicata, where the region has just twenty-eight kilometres of coast, along the Gulf of Policastro, is Maratea, an interesting little town perched on the side of Monte San Biagio; it has an excellent fish restaurant by the sea at Maratea Santavenere, called Ristorante Cesarino, and another at a nearby hotel called the Villa Cheta.

While the Porto di Maratea has a railway station, Rivello, about twenty-three kilometres inland, in the Valle di Noce, can only be reached by road. By tradition, people say that Rivello is laid out in the form of an enormous dragon. Others think it looks like a person stretched out on a mattress: the church of San Nicola is the head, Santa Barbara the knees and Santa Maria del Poggio the feet; the two rows of houses running the length of the hill are the arms. Narrow streets, shallow staircases and red pantiled roofs are the dominant characteristics of Rivello.

Entering Basilicata from the north, the first hill town of any interest is Melfi. It is dominated by a huge castle that Emperor Charles v gave to the Doria princes in the sixteenth century. Now the seat of the Melfi National Museum, it contains the area's archaeological treasures. To the south is Monte Vulture, an extinct volcano that gave two important Lucanian wines their name: Moscato del Vulture, a white wine, and, from

A fine view of Castelmezzano from Pietrapertosa.

the red grapes of the Aglianico vines of Greek origin, the Aglianico del Vulture, which is ruby red in colour and smells of strawberries and raspberries.

There are at least five types of Aglianico wine, from sparkling Aglianico del Vulture Spumante to Aglianico 'Dolce, a fragrant red dessert wine. Ordinary red Aglianico is best drunk with local things like *cavitella*, a pasta with turnip tops, such as you get at Melfi's Ristorante La Fattoria at Lago Pertusillo, or with homemade *strascinate*, a pasta with a sauce of tomatoes, fresh pork sausage, basil, onions and chilli.

In Basilicata nearly all rural families have a constant supply of pig meat in a variety of forms on their domestic menus. Most have at least one huge porker. In particularly straightened circumstances they kill it, with much celebrating, and then prepare every bit of the

*P*ietrapertosa high in its rocky domain.

unfortunate animal in some way for the table. Carlo Levi was present when the sows of Gagliano, near Stigliano, were castrated by the pig doctor in order to make them fatter and more tender to eat. Such was the importance of the pig to the family that they were prepared to see it staked to the ground and operated on while it screamed with terror, then watch while it was stitched up again, fully conscious, and the wound was sealed with a surgical knot. The operation, which lasted three to four minutes, was accompanied by 'the sign of the cross … and a prayer to the Madonna of Viggiano …'.

One favourite pudding produced nearly everywhere in Basilicata is called *pastiere*, a sort of black pudding. It is made using pig's blood, rice, cocoa, grated chocolate, coffee, cinnamon, carnation cloves, sugar and raisins, and is baked in the oven using pork fat. Some Lucanian dishes only appeal to specialized or individual

*T*he church of San Francisco in Pietrapertosa (top right).
(Above) *Another view of Pietrapertosa from Castelmezzano.*

palates. On street stalls in the bigger towns of Basilicata, on market day or during festivals, you can buy *pezzente salami*, made for *pezzente* (beggars). All the bits that butchers generally throw away – lungs, livers, nerve ends – are bundled together, seasoned with garlic and pepper, and then made into salami. There is another salami called *lucanega* or *lucaneca*, which is said to have been made in Basilicata since Roman times. *Soppressata*, a large blood sausage sometimes containing ginger or red peppers, is another. This can be eaten raw, grilled or fried, or alternatively dried or smoked.

Basilicata was never very fertile or productive, and not much grows in the arid lunar landscape of the *calanchi* district in the southeast, around the ruined town of Craco. The parched country here is more North African than Italian. Even less can be coaxed from the rocky dolomitic hills near Castelmezzano and Pietrapertosa, south-east of Potenza.

Castelmezzano and Pietrapertosa are two of the highest towns in the Lucanian Dolomites. Bizarrely twisted rocks and peaks shelter both towns, which face each other across a deep ravine, and there is only one road to each. From the main Potenza–Metaponto route, which runs through the Basento valley to the sea, the road winds up towards both towns, divides, then approaches each separately. It is a hazardous journey, the most serious obstacle in which, apart from the hairpin bends and the precipitous drop to one side, is always a shepherd and his flock of sheep. Not quite the legendary 'curly-haired striplings' dressed in skins, spoken of so admiringly by Norman Douglas in his book *In Calabria*, these shepherds arrive at the pastures nowadays in shining Fiats, park them in the shade, then while away their day leaning against the roadside fence, cracking nuts and listening to the radio while their flocks wander about in nearby steeply sloping fields.

The old road to these towns still exists; under the broom bushes and the thick wild grass, it can still be seen in part, dilapidated and abandoned and made of small regularly shaped stone blocks. Donkeys and carts once laboured up it, slipping in the rain. Today's road is tarred and just wide enough for two cars to pass one another.

The Castelmezzano road vanishes into a tunnel, emerges directly in front of the town, skirting its base, and then immediately enters the main Piazza Caiazzo. As with many of the southern hill towns, the central piazza is like the town's drawing room. It is a cul-de-sac, the end of the road up to the town; beyond it the streets are too narrow for cars. Piazza Caiazzo is also the mechanic's workshop and a saleroom for itinerant merchants. Along one of its sides is a row of metal seats, each one occupied by a greying unshaven old man in a handsome corduroy suit. On Sundays salesmen fill the square with tables covered with pirate music cassettes, tapestries of the Virgin, sunglasses and hideously misogynistic pornographic literature. The younger *Castelmezzani* mill about here in an idle fashion, toying with items, buying nothing and gossiping with their friends.

Piazza Caiazzo also has the town's only water pump. In the summer, when water is scarce,

*N*arrow streets and shallow staircases are two dominant features of Rivello.

rather than line up for ages waiting for water to emerge at the appointed hour, the women abandon their plastic bottles in a line in front of the tap; they then go about their daily chores until their turn at the tap. Someone's child gives a signal and each woman rushes back in turn to fill her bottles. In August they have an hour to do this. Their plastic bottles trail down the sloping square, mingling with dogs, the wheels of cars and a nun with her charge of infants going into the church overlooking the square for their daily catechism class. Sunday car washes also take place here, much to the annoyance of the pedestrians.

On one side of the square is the belvedere, from which you can look down over a sharp 500-metre drop, past the town's last houses and their terraced plots, to the rocky valley below. In the past this vantage point was significant. With an excellent view to the south, watch could be kept over any threatening movement far below. From the north, from the wide Basento River valley that cuts deep into Basilicata from the Ionian Sea, Castelmezzano doesn't exist: you can't see it from the Potenza–Metaponto road. Hidden behind a row of sharp dolomitic needles, it had the best of both worlds. In the Middle Ages, perhaps even earlier, the highest of the rocky outcrops behind the town were turned into lookout posts, and steps were gouged into them so that a small boy could be sent up to keep watch. This natural fortress is today covered in long grass and wild flowers. Old women in black climb up to it, leading their goats, and bring back clumps of wild herbs in bundles on their heads.

The arrival of my car, with its Milanese number plates, in Piazza Caiazzo was greeted with looks of complete incredulity from the local population. Everyone stared. Not stares of hostility but of curiosity as they murmured quietly to themselves: why come here? The truth is that, although Castelmezzano has no great cathedral and no special works of art

indicative of a glorious past, it does have all the rudiments of a working hill town that is still fully inhabited by a mix of young and old. Ancient houses line the narrow streets. Barns and stables under the little houses are still used by the family's livestock, and outside the houses are small whitewashed ovens, one to a group of four or five dwellings, which are still used each week to bake bread.

Most people in Castelmezzano still work on the land; their preoccupations are earthbound. The *nonne* (grandmothers), who also live in the family home, deal with the chickens and the goat. These ancient women, nimble even at nearly ninety years of age, spend their day pottering about the chicken coops, dressed in black, heads covered with scarves, all their attention focused on the minutiae of stable life. While their husbands are sitting in the Piazza Caiazzo picking their teeth, their sons and daughters-in-law are out hoeing the allotments around the base of the town. In the evenings brushwood is collected and brought back on a donkey, or tied up with string and carried back to the house on the women's heads for stacking. Activities here are timeless, and concessions to the twentieth century are incidental: some families have tiny Piaggio vans, which are the mechanized equivalents of the family donkey; most have radios and televisions.

*P*antile rooftops (above) *lead the way towards Rivello's church of San Michele dei Greci.*
(Overleaf): *An archetypal view of an Italian hill town as it spreads across the surrounding countryside.*

Pietrapertosa is slightly bigger than Castelmezzano. It lies on either side of other, stranger, needle-like rock formations. The road sweeps into the town on the north side, underneath a heavy rocky overhang, then enters the main body of Pietrapertosa from its highest point. Steep alleys and lanes weave their way downhill, past interesting little *palazzetti* with carved doorways and little wrought-iron balconies, to the church of San Francesco on a ridge opposite the town. San Francesco is a repository of Lucanian art. Apart from a polyptych behind the altar by Pietrafesa, the most notable local painter, there is a rogues' gallery of plaster and plastic saints lining the nave. Each one, local saints, national saints, the Virgin and some angels, is dressed in real clothing, some of it fairly ancient, worked in gold thread and embroidery, and some of rather more mundane, yellowing linen. Most wear medals, jewellery and even shoes. Others looked faintly ridiculous in modern spectacles and flipflops, and an uncontrollable urge to laugh made me leave the church, bringing to a halt my investigations.

In these little towns, far from mainstream events and, until fairly recently, not even connected to the main highways except by small rough tracks, the boundaries between Christian worship and the left-overs of pagan ritual are so vague as to be almost indistinguishable. The May First Communion Day at Pietrapertosa exhibits something of this. Early in the morning on the chosen day, the surrounding hills are full of people out picking the yellow flowers of the broom bushes, poppies, wild roses and scented herbs. These are taken home and broken up, petal by petal, to be used later in the day in the First Communion procession, as confetti or as carpeting along the route.

The processional route weaves through the principal streets and past the town's shrines. Petals are strewn on the ground in front of the shrines and outside the doors of the First Communicants' homes. In the Via Garibaldi is a little early baroque chapel whose main doors, at the top of two steps, open directly onto the street. A cross of petals is laid out in the road in front of the doorway, while smaller crosses are laid at the end of each step. A circle of rose and broom petals closes off the approach to the building, barring anyone from entering. There is a pagan magic to this scene and I felt compelled to draw back, leaving the chapel unexplored. Other geometric patterns in the circle are inexplicable, and an old crone seated on a chair close by ensures that they remain unviolated until the procession has passed.

The route is further decorated by lengths of cloth hanging from the first floor windows of nearby houses. In the past, in the Middle Ages or when Pietrapertosa was a more important place, these would have been tapestries or heraldic banners. Now any old sheet will do, or a bright tablecloth or curtain slung out of the window. The festive spirit survives nonetheless. The procession consists of an interesting local mix of people straggling by to the church of San Francesco: macho *carabinieri* leading small daughters dressed as brides, old farmhands in white shirts rigid with starch, and gaggles of elderly Pietrapertosa females with scrubbed ruddy faces, dressed in black and clutching bunches of wild flowers. I felt out of place until somebody thrust a handful of petals into my hand. These I flung at an angel attired in white polyester as she rushed by, churchbound, on the back of her brother's motorbike.

As in the rest of Italy, occasions such as this require other festive elements. Food is one important ingredient, wine another. There are no specific delicacies for this particular event, but at Christmas Pietrapertosa's most typical restaurant, Le Rocche in the Via Nazionale, serves traditional things like *pettole*, which are fritters cooked with honey and wine, and at Easter *pannaredd*, which are pastry eggs decorated with sweets.

The Potenza–Metaponto road winds on through the mountains to Pisticci, about thirty-five kilometres from the sea. There is another road parallel to this, a smaller country road which goes through the hill towns of Tricarico, Grassano, Grottole and Miglionico. From Grassano to Miglionico the countryside alters dramatically, throwing up rock formations called *calanchi*. Although Pisticci has its own station, the nearest rail terminal to any of the others is at Miglionico. Stop there and buses will take you to any other part of the countryside, though the convoluted gyrations of the country roads may take ages to negotiate.

Pisticci is a gleaming white hill town, its most characteristic feature its rows of terraced houses with pointed roofs and brightly painted doorways. It is a vibrant agricultural centre with a daily market. Here women wearing the town's traditional costume, a long black nun-like skirt and huge white collar, confidently shop alongside more modern females in jeans and miniskirts. They seem strangely incongruous among the household appliances, buying detergents and electric irons.

The women of southern Italy practise one other important ritual of daily life. When a person dies, female relations gather around the

Whitewashed, sunbleached cottages line the cool shadowy alleys which are generally deserted at midday in Apulia.

body and 'lament' their death. The origins of this are antique; at Pisticci there is no mention of the Virgin or the saints in the 'lament', so it is very possible that it pre-dates the Christian era. At the moment of death, once the eyelids have been pulled down, the women of the dead person's family, plus a few other highly skilled mourners among their neighbours and friends, begin to screech in an agonized and unholy expression of grief. They scratch at their faces, tear their hair, bang their heads against the wall and contort their bodies in a variety of expressions of pain and suffering as they move in slow motion around the room. They unload their sorrow onto the world, then, altering course, begin a melodic whine, desperate in character, which leads to a state of near hysteria. This can last for up to forty-eight hours. Repetitious and primitive, their caterwauling is not an expression of sorrow that courts comforting. Instead it is a selfish expression of fury at the death (if it is a man) of the breadwinner.

One lament, typical of Pisticci even now, translates thus: 'My … [husband's name], treasure of your wife, who died suddenly, treasure of your wife, oh! what precious hands you had. What toil you have made with those

hands, treasure of your wife. And now I must tell you what I have put in your coffin, treasure of your wife: two shirts, one new and one patched, treasure of your wife; a cloth to clean your face in the next world, treasure of your wife; two pairs of underpants, one new and one with a patch on the seat; and then I have put your pipe, treasure of your wife. And now who must I send to you with your cigar in the other world, treasure of your wife?' There is nothing Christian about this. It is a purely pagan concern with the well-being of the dead in the afterlife.

Basilicata is one of the most riveting areas of Italy. But it does require a lot of time in order to witness and understand the daily rituals of the population, and to explore its ancient untouched towns and countryside.

A P U L I A

Apulia is the only region of Italy that matches Sicily in the variety of its cultural inheritance. Closer to Greece than any other part of the Italian peninsula, most of it was colonized by the Greeks, the earliest, the most powerful and the longest-lasting influence on the area. It was favoured by the Romans because it was a convenient disembarkation point from which to conquer the east, so its ports were enriched by trade and a cosmopolitan influx of people. The power of Byzantine rule was a major force until the tenth century, after which Apulia became an important part of the dominions of Frederick II of Hohenstaufen. As ruler of Sicily, Holy Roman Emperor and King of Jerusalem, Frederick provided Apulia with its own Golden Age. It became rich, powerful and cosmopolitan, with flourishing artistic, architectural and culinary traditions, the remnants of which survive today in one form or another.

Most of Apulia is a flat plain. It is not an area massively endowed with hill towns, although the

The church of Santa Maria Maddalena (far left) *with its multi-coloured glazed terracotta cupola and the rose window of the Duomo* (left).

great island of steel-grey rock which rises from the plain to the north, the Gargano mountain range, does have a sprinkling of hilltop communities scattered about its extremities. Jutting out into the Adriatic Sea, this is said to be the most scenic stretch of coastline between Venice and the tip of the Calabrian peninsula.

The important hill towns of the Gargano are Monte Sant'Angelo and San Giovanni Rotondo, both, throughout their histories, a tramping ground for holy men. Monte Sant'Angelo lay at the end of the Via Sacra Longobardum, a pilgrimage route which began at Benevento in Campania, on the other side of the Monti della Daunia, the mountain range which separates Campania from Apulia; the route then passed through San Marco in Lamis, in the centre of the Gargano promontory, and San Giovanni Rotondo.

At Monte Sant'Angelo, a whitewashed warren of steep steps, tunnels and passages under small, low buildings, is a sanctuary – a basilica – built over a large deep cavern full of altars, which is impregnated with a damp fusty smell. This was a holy site long before the advent of Christianity. Having been a revered spot sacred to an oracle, it was dedicated to St Michael the Archangel in the fifth century. The veiled women murmuring prayers and shuffling about in its darkened recesses today, lighting candles and praying on plastic rosaries, are the latest in a long line of pilgrims who once entered the holy hole in the ground on their knees. The more illustrious of these included St Thomas Aquinas and St Francis. Most people don't prostrate themselves before St Michael the Archangel in this manner any more. There is no time. Affecting scenes of reverence are rudely interrupted when the doors to the sanctuary are slammed shut at 12.30.

From Monte Sant'Angelo the SS 272 winds east towards San Giovanni Rotondo, which stands on a plateau beneath the Gargano's highest peak. This was the home of a latter-day

saint, Padre Pio da Pietralcina, who received the stigmata, and was able to appear at ecclesiastical discussion groups in Rome while still sleeping in his bed in the Gargano. His particular abilities drew, and continue to draw, crowds of pilgrims: although he died in 1968, they still flood the town. They used to come to hear Padre Pio speak. Now they crowd the twenty hotels and put their sick into a very large new hospital, the Fiorello La Guardia Hospital, where they await some manifestation of the Padre's miracle-working.

In August there is a *Festa dell'Ospite*, a sort of Guest's Festival, at San Giovanni, with exhibitions and activities relating to the town's folklore. Most people take part, with the help of a great deal of the local Orta Nova, a red or rosé wine from the surrounding province.

There are some interesting little churches here, for example the fourteenth-century Sant' Onofrio and a little rotonda that gives the town its name. The origins of this building are rather obscure, though by tradition it was constructed on the ruins of a temple dedicated to Jupiter.

These little towns lie scattered about the Gargano forests – primeval woodlands of beech, oak and pine. The biggest, the Foresta Umbra, becomes less dense around Monte Sant'Angelo and peters out completely towards the south, as the landscape is transformed into gulleys and rivulets which give way to the plain of the once malaria-ridden Tavoliere. Beyond, Apulia is engulfed by the sluggish low-lying hills of the Murge.

One of the principal towns of the Murge is Ostuni. Another is Minervo Murge, a farming centre in an elevated position on the edge of the Murge Alta. In the Murge Tarentine is Grottaglie, a major centre for ceramics, close to Taranto. Ceramic adornments enliven the buildings of this little town, and in August each year there is an important exhibition-cum-market of ceramics of all types.

Ostuni is possibly the most interesting of

these three towns. It lies on the edge of a strange landscape divided by ancient crumbling stone walls, which enclose huge old twisted olive trees. It is also dotted with peculiar conical dwellings and huts called *trulli*, circular stone bunkers of hybrid architectural origins, part African, part Arabic and part Greek. From the Zona dei Trulli, the upland plateau between Ostuni and Alberobello where these buildings are concentrated, Ostuni rises like a phantom in the summer haze. Dazzlingly white, its houses cover three small rocky knolls, which overlook the Adriatic and swoop down to the coast to the north-east.

The old town of Ostuni, enclosed in part by the remains of the Aragonese wall, is a maze of narrow streets that wind their way in a spiral up to the fifteenth-century Duomo. Three ogival doors look out onto the Largo Arcidiacono Teodoro Trinchera and the little stone bridge connecting the two sides of the Episcopal Palace. On the way up to the Duomo, past the baroque church of Santa Maria Maddalena, with its multi-coloured cupola, bland whitewashed façades are punctuated by richly sculpted portals and balconies. This particular street, the Via Cattedrale, is the old town's main thoroughfare. It widens and narrows at whim, squeezes between blinding white buildings more Arabic-looking than Italian, and eventually fades away into numerous blank alleyways.

The Via Cattedrale has a number of interesting shops. In particular there is the Antichità e i Fischietti di Peppino Carella, which sells antique ceramics decorated in the local vernacular style – spongeware pasta dishes and tin-glazed jugs – and ancient *cassone*, some emblazoned with the arms of long defunct families, others painted with biblical scenes and passages from local legends. This is a rare shop in southern Italy, an area where most antiques of this kind are removed by dealers who comb whole districts, and then send their 'finds' to the antique markets of Arezzo and Milan.

On cool summer evenings black-clad women sit out at little tables in the lanes and side streets of the old town, and roll, cut and shape pasta while chatting to their neighbours or passing comments to strangers walking by. Pasta made like this is usually quite coarse, though it is much better at soaking up sauces. The type most commonly found in Apulia is called *orecchiette*, 'little ears', made by rolling the thumb over bits of pasta against a board. It is usually served with tomato sauce or with turnip tops and olive oil. Another favourite dish is *orecchiette con cime e acciughe*, with turnip tops and anchovies.

Apart from *orecchiette* (*recchie* for short), the women also make other pasta shapes, the strangest of which are *cavatieddi* which look like little shells, *strascenate*, *chiancarelle*, *troccolli*, *mignuicchie* and *pociacche*. The people of Apulia have a particular passion for pasta. Ever since the Spanish tried to tax it in the seventeenth century, after which savage riots broke out all over the region, pasta of every shape and size has been central to their diet.

A beaten metal door in Ostuni.

LAZIO

BOMARZO · VITORCHIANO · BAGNAIA
CAPRAROLA · TUSCANIA

Lazio, Latium to the ancient Romans, is often rudely dismissed as the land surrounding Rome. It is true that the fortunes of the inhabitants of the country towns outside the Eternal City depended to a very large extent on those of Rome, and on the rise and fall of the Roman aristocracy, on whose estates many of these towns lay. But while this is no longer true today, the effect of draining these towns of their resources over the centuries has meant that many of them have taken longer to adjust to the twentieth century than might otherwise have been the case. Feudal families kept the land in check, and the popes trawled it for building materials and water, so that nowadays Lazio is unique in Central Italy in having to rely on the government for financial assistance for development.

The country towns were islands in the middle of vast estates. Ones like Caprarola were completely subordinate to the whims of the Farnese family, who owned it. Caprarola's appearance was altered dramatically so that it would align with a new Farnese palace there. And the old town of Bagnaia became simply an adjunct to the Villa Lante, the property of Cardinal Gambera: when the Cardinal came to visit it he would house his retinue in the town, the pavilions of the villa being rather too small for everybody.

Other towns, like Vitorchiano, seem to have relished their role as satellites in Rome's constellation. In fact the town had a tradition of subservience to Rome. Even the Porta Romana gets its name not from the fact that it was built in ancient Roman days (which it wasn't) but from the fact that it faces the Eternal City.

Today the quickest way to enter Lazio from the north is via the Autostrada del Sole, the A1, which connects Florence with Rome. The first part of the Lazio section rushes dramatically between the Monti Cimini and the Monti Sabini, passing on the way clusters of small towns of unprepossessing appearance, crammed on top of large island-like clusters of rock in a sea of woodland and scrub. These towns have a strongly defensive character, and their purple-black buildings are dour and watchful.

Bomarzo is one of these, perhaps the most interesting. It lies very close to the Umbrian

The back wall of the outermost houses of Bomarzo (above) once doubled up as the town's protective wall. Beyond Bomarzo, on a bank of the distant Monte Cimino, is the little hilltown of Soriano.

border, in the northern extremity of Lazio, about seventy kilometres from Rome. This little town lay undiscovered and ignored for centuries, until, about twenty-five years ago, it was 'rediscovered' by Salvador Dali, who was fascinated by the Giardino dei Mostri, the Monster Garden, outside the town at the base of the hill. Dozens of books have discussed the garden in detail, and I will confine myself here to a description of Bomarzo itself.

It is built of a kind of tufa, called *peperino*, a volcanic stone which is fairly common in this area. From afar the dark hulk of this little town is indistinguishable from the rock in which it is embedded. A wall surrounds the highest and most ancient part of it, and at one time it was completely impregnable. Below, outside the gates and at the bottom of a steep ramp, is the newer part of Bomarzo; in this case new means that it isn't, for the most part, medieval, like the upper town, but was constructed two or three hundred years later. It is much less interesting visually than the upper town, but since it has the one and only bar it is hard to avoid.

A huge ramshackle gate, buried in a wall of massive cut stone, opens into the upper town and the narrow main street, which is only about two metres across. This leads into a maze of other alleys and damp mildewy passages, and

The butcher (above) – where you might buy tripe to which the locals are rather partial. (Right) The Porta Romana in the hefty wall protecting Vitorchiano.

eventually ends in the tightly enclosed Piazza del Duomo. The Duomo, rather grandly named, is, in reality, a small church, with a miniature baroque horse-shoe stair leading, even more grandly, to its main entrance. The façade of the building has been washed the colour of apricot so that it enlivens the black heart of the town, whose little shuttered houses have outside stairs with wrought-iron handrails.

Bomarzo is an eerie place, and my hobnailed boots penetrated its silence with what seemed to me to be an earth-shattering violence. Parts of the old castle are now private flats, but the most interesting bit of it can be visited if you can be bothered to find someone who knows how to find the person who can tell you which family keeps the key. Inside, in the main chamber, is an impressive ceiling fresco by Anton Angelo Bonifazi, a pupil of Pietro da Cortona. It ought to be seen before it collapses; the entire building is incredibly run down and the painting under threat of obliteration.

Vitorchiano, just a few kilometres to the west, is the same colour as Bomarzo. Much bigger, much livelier and much more enthusiastic about life, its centre seems to have been burrowed out of a single large lump of tufa. The

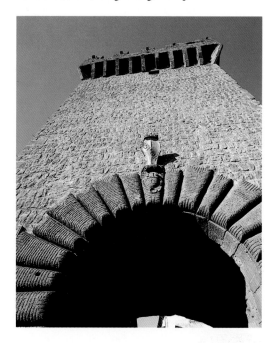

walls, the streets and the paving stones are all the same dusty purple. Vitorchiano even has an annual exhibition which celebrates the existence of the *peperino* building stone. For a week, starting on the last Sunday in June, a whole series of local cultural events – primarily exhibitions and workshops – take place, most of which revolve around the working of this stone by local craftsmen. As a side attraction there is a *taverna medievale*, a medieval tavern, which serves food based on ancient local recipes.

Vitorchiano is a very ancient place. Everything about it points to its lifelong loyalty to Rome. According to a medieval legend, this stems from the time when a man called Marzio ran to Rome to warn the Senate of an impending attack on the Campidoglio by a band of Etruscans. Having passed on this information, the man promptly dropped dead from septicaemia; a thorn had entered his foot on the way to Rome and he hadn't had time to remove

it. (The well known classical statue of the 'Spinario', kept in the Capitoline Museum in Rome, is said to represent Marzio himself.) For this the Senate rewarded Vitorchiano with the title '*città fedele*', 'faithful city'. Even today you see the Roman SPQR on the municipal coat of arms. The inscription '*Romano imperio summa fidelitas*' appears everywhere on the lintels of door and windows, and there is even a Roman wolf or two suckling Romulus and Remus, carved, in shallow relief, on stones set into the ancient crumbling walls of some of the houses.

So faithful was the town to Rome in later years that in 1267 the Romans honoured the people with the name 'Fedeli di Vitorchiano'. Since then the town has been entitled to supply ceremonial mace-bearers and guardsmen to keep the Campidoglio under surveillance; even today, on official occasions, the Fedeli di Vitorchiano stand beside the banners of Rome in their costumes designed by Michelangelo.

Bomarzo is dominated by the Castello Orsino, one of the feudal bases of the ancient Orsini family.

The Porta Romana frames the entrance to the town. Framing the Porta Romana is the town's geriatric male population, sitting about in the cool shade of the huge old chestnuts by the fountain, gossiping and smoking, unshaven in their country suits, which are patched and threadbare. A hefty wall stretches out on either side of the gate, protecting Vitorchiano on one side, while the sheer height of the rock on which the town sits defends the rest of it. The houses themselves seem to grow out of this massive rocky lump, and in fact the basements of many of them are actually cut out of the rock itself; above, narrow wooden balconies and flimsy washing lines thrown from the windows are suspended dramatically above the drop to the water and bushes below. These outside walls have no proper definition; you can't tell from afar where one house begins and the next one ends. They seem rather like buttresses and fortifications,

The watch tower at Bagnaia.

which are meant to protect the little squares and streets within, while their little shuttered windows are the only contact the town has with the outside world.

Unlike Bomarzo, Vitorchiano's population is actually swelling. Perhaps its proximity to Viterbo (only eight kilometres away) makes it a popular place. Its houses are being restored, and, while laws govern alterations to their exteriors, their interiors are being efficiently updated, often for the first time in their entire histories. Apart from the old women sitting out on the steps, peeling vegetables or preparing pasta among the geraniums, and the stray kittens playing in the sun, there are plenty of younger sons and daughters happy to carry on living in their urban ancestral homes.

The actual *centro storico* is so small, and so tightly packed with tiny houses piled on top of one another, that the way people live here is

*Bagnaia is made up of narrow, ancient streets straggling
down the rocky crag which is the town's base.*

affected quite dramatically. The town's squares and streets become the sitting rooms of the houses, while the houses themselves remain places for eating and sleeping only. So cramped is Vitorchiano that if one person wants to tune in to Diana Ross on the radio in the north-east of the town, and others decide to do the same in the south or west, anyone in the street has the benefit of magnified multiphonic music for which the stone heart of the town provides ample echo. This didn't seem out of place to me. On the contrary, it assured me that the town was alive and kicking.

A wander through the streets of Vitorchiano is fraught with minor hazards arising from vigorous domestic industry. At intervals throughout the day, dust is swept from the landings of the staircase approaches to the houses. These are at eye level, or mouth level, and, if you happen to be a stranger to Vitorchiano, a quick sweep of the landing is a good excuse for a nosey housewife to have a look at you and wonder what you're doing there. If it's not dust in your face then it's large drips of water down your neck from yet another article of newly washed clothing which has just been flung across the washing line suspended across the street; you can be observed from an upper window more effectively and more discreetly, and for longer, and the looks are just as curious.

At intervals along these routes, as you cross the town's succession of three little *piazze* – della Trinità, Agnese and Roma – and pass by the town's *chiesette* (little churches), like the Renaissance Sant'Antonio Abate and the fourteenth-century Santissima Trinità, you find old shrines dedicated to the Virgin nailed to the wall. These occasionally take the form of a fresco, but nowadays they are more likely to be plastic images, set in a glass case and accompanied by a derelict candle. They are generally covered in dust and cobwebs, and nobody really knows any longer why they were ever put in this particular place. Certainly nobody cares, and only the old women seem to bother to put fresh flowers on the shelf in front of them. Still, they are landmarks of a sort and you can use them as meeting points: 'See you at the Virgin's at 2.00 ...'.

There are only a couple of restaurants in Vitorchiano. At the corner of the Via Ariosto and the Via Arringa is the Bar/Ristorante La Grotticella, and around the corner, still in the Via Ariosto, the Osteria dell'Arco. Both are the kind of place where you'll be told what has been freshly made that day. You'll be expected to order from that selection, and if you don't the service will be erratic thereafter. Both of them are very unpretentious places, *trattorie* in fact, where you might get a broth containing *quadrucci* (little squares of homemade pasta) to start with, or else some sort of pasta dish on its own. The next course will arrive suffused in garlic and olive oil, and will most probably have something to do with offal. These vigorously flavoured favourites might be a dish of beans with pigskin, or oxtail stewed in wine. There might be *trippa alla Romana* (tripe with sauce and *pecorino* cheese, made from sheep's milk, grated over it); on the other hand, there might be fried brains with artichokes. Less mind-boggling perhaps are the *involtini di manzo alla Romana* (slices of beef rolled up with various things inside them) and *saltimbocca* (veal slices,

The gardens of the Ville Lante, including the Fountain of Pegasus, were laid out by Vignola.

raw ham and sage leaves held together with a toothpick).

If that doesn't force you to sit motionless for the rest of the day, then the local wine definitely will. The Viterbo area is known for its white Est Est Est wine – more famous perhaps for the quantity produced than for the quality. Unassuming and easy to drink with any type of cooking, its name stems from the fact that there was once a servant of a travelling prelate who was instructed to write *Est* on the door of a household in which he had found a good wine. The prelate, keen on wine, would then know where to stop. At Montefiascone, just north of Viterbo, the servant came across a really good one, so he wrote *Est Est Est* on the door. The religious old soak, so enchanted by this find, drank himself to death on vast quantities of it and had to be buried in the local churchyard. Needless to say, the wine went from strength to strength, though history doesn't relate what happened to the servant.

This area also produces the red Aleatico wine and a great many others, which will be found in abundance in the grander restaurants of Viterbo – at the Leon d'Oro or the Tuscia. Viterbo is in fact a good place to base yourself for a visit to the area, and has quite a number of hotels. It also has a railway station from which you can reach both Bomarzo and Vitorchiano.

A couple of kilometres outside Viterbo is Bagnaia, a little town rather like Vitorchiano in appearance. Built out of the same *peperino* stone, it sits at the extremity of a spur which juts out of the hillside. Like Vitorchiano, this was an example of judicious planning because only one end of it had to be fortified. Today the only remains of these fortifications, apart from the old archway surrounding the original position of the gate, is a cylindrical crenellated tower which dominates everything around it.

In front is the Piazza XX Settembre, which separates the old town from the new – new because the later part was laid out and con-structed in the sixteenth century. The two couldn't be more different: the old town is full of idiosyncratic angles, old passages and worn steps, while the new is made up of straight angular roads which fan out of the piazza and lead directly up the hill towards the town's single most important attraction, the Villa Lante, now open to the public. In days gone by, when the Bishops of Viterbo took their holidays at the Villa Lante, the juxtaposition of old town and villa must have been bizarre – the one a lowly, austere medieval rabbit warren, the other an opulent and aristocratic masterpiece of garden design.

Created for Cardinal Gambara, the Villa Lante's enclosed gardens are considered Vignola's most important garden design. At the centre of the garden, and to the left of the old hunting park of the Cardinal Riario, who owned the estate in the fifteenth century, are two separate pavilions which are linked by a ramp which ascends gently to an upper terrace. These, the villa's accommodation, were probably found to be the most convenient way of providing more house room without disturbing the existing plan of the grounds. In front, on a wide flat terrace is a water parterre in the centre of which four blackened figures, the Moors, hold up the device of Cardinal Montalto, who succeeded Cardinal Gambera and who completed the garden. In the water are little stone

*N*obody remembers why the Virgin is commemorated in this particular location (above); only the old women leave flowers here for her. Vitorchiano (overleaf) is built of a dusty purple peperino, a volcanic stone fairly common in north-east Lazio.

'boats' full of geraniums which seem to float. This is the Fontana dei Mori and all around it are formal parterres of cut box hedges, still beautifully kept, and little gravel paths.

The use of water in these gardens was perfected to the point at which it has become an art form. It is the stylized interpretation of a natural phenomenon and in essence was the model for many later gardens. It also contains some hazardous jets of water, *giochi d'acqua*, jokes or trick fountains, which could be operated so that they drenched whoever was passing by. These no longer work, or so they say. The mechanisms may just be very fragile, and to wet passers-by may not be a very positive way of attracting visitors.

Bagnaia today is a very lively place, perhaps because it has become almost a suburb of Viterbo and is very easy to reach. The concept of the piazza as drawing room is nowhere more prevalent than here in the Piazza XX Settembre. Youths from Viterbo come out from the city centre on their motorbikes to hang out at the Bar Centrale Club Firecat, with its *al fresco* seating, black marble interior and loud music. On Sundays a man wheels a cart containing a huge

carcass of roast pig on a spit out into the piazza; from it, for 1500 lire, you can buy chunks of *porchetta*, roast meat and salty crackling. If the *passeggiata* ever really takes place at Bagnaia, then this is its location. Cars, scooters, prams, dogs and an inconvenient traffic light in the centre of the piazza contribute to the chaotic confusion of this, the salon of Bagnaia.

Signposts from Viterbo will also direct you to Caprarola. A winding country road runs through the Monti Cimini and skirts the right hand shore of the Lago di Vico, which fills the crater of an extinct volcano, now fringed with the remnants of the Cimino forest, then zig zags its way inland again to the town. André Maurel, novelist and Italophile, came here in 1913 and noted that the landscape was 'a confusion of miniature mountains ... contorted by the fire within ... thrown up to left and right, haphazardly. It's a mess, a muddle of hills ...'.

In the midst of the ructions is Caprarola, dominated by the red mastodontic edifice of the Palazzo Farnese, whose pentagon shape rises dramatically from the rustic landscape all around. The actual town below the palace was carefully re-shaped so that its main street was aligned with the entrance forecourt to the building, providing a theatrical approach for visitors. No doubt Vignola, the architect, was aware of the imperiousness of his creation; undoubtedly the Farnese family, his clients, were too, and no doubt they loved the fact that there were now two towns, one for them and one for the people, so large was their new country palace.

To obtain maximum effect, and to see Caprarola as Vignola intended you to see it, you must approach from Monterosi, which lies on the Viterbo–Rome road about thirteen kilometres south of Caprarola. This, in the past, was the shortest route from Rome, and it connected with the long main street that Vignola literally rammed through the measly medieval village of Caprarola, destroying a number of houses and necessitating the construction of

The meeting of the two worlds: the aristocratic Farnese residence and the poor scruffy houses of their subordinates.

two new bridges, which linked the three hills upon which the town and palace are built.

While Giorgio Vasari and Montaigne came here in the fifteenth century – the former muttering about the genius of Vignola, the latter extolling the noble virtues of the House of Farnese and its resident pope, Paul III – in the nineteenth century it was host to Bernard Berenson, Lord Berners, Gabriele D'Annunzio and Robert Trevelyan. During this period it was rented by a wealthy American, Florence Baldwin, from Alfonso di Borbone, who was in exile in France. Her occupation continued well into the twentieth century, during which time André Maurel was her guest. His description of the palace and of his stay in it, descsribed in *Paysages d'Italie*, is interesting because it illuminates how this huge palace was adapted to early twentieth-century living. The dining room, according to Florence Baldwin's butler, could seat up to four hundred guests quite comfortably, while all the little cubby holes in the massive walls were converted to contain lavatories and lifts. All this is in great contrast to the 'wretched and dirty' town that André Maurel saw out of the window.

Looking over the edge of the very last of the bridges, you see the little houses bundled beneath in an unruly near-subterranean jumble. It is no longer 'wretched and dirty', and I found it very satisfying to note that it was the town that had had the last laugh: while the Farnese are extinct and their palace lies empty, the town continues to exist and to thrive as an agricultural centre.

Caprarola is a very popular Sunday lunch venue for visiting Romans, who come to dine on *cinghiale* (wild boar) or *lepre in agrodolce* (sweet and sour hare), a dish once found only in papal kitchens during the Renaissance, and now available at some local family-run hostelries in and around this area, including the Trattoria/Bar del Cimino, just below the piazza at the top of the main street.

From Viterbo you can also get to Tuscania by bus or car. Twenty-four kilometres away, in the opposite direction to Caprarola, it lies in a strange Afro-grassland style of landscape, quite eerie, empty and very ancient; most of it was toppled by an earthquake in 1971. Tuscania was once the site of an Etruscan necropolis, and the town's Museo Archeologico is immensely interesting. The churches of San Pietro and Santa Maria Maggiore, both of which were begun in the 700s, and then added to in the eleventh and twelfth centuries, are fascinating repositories of the cultural artefacts of the ages. The courtyard in front of San Pietro is cluttered with reclining Etruscan matrons, who once formed the lids of stone tombs, and bits of classical sculpture lying wherever history, archeologists or the earthquake tossed them. Both churches must be seen—silent and dark, San Pietro on its hill overlooking the countryside and Santa Maria Maggiore on the edge of an odd bamboo grove. The texture of the centuries on the walls of both buildings, the sculpture, the frescoes, the mosaics and the architecture induce a certain melancholy if you are the only visitor (which is often the case).

The houses of Caprarola crammed beneath the Palazzo Farnese.

ABRUZZO

COCULLO · CASTROVALVA · ANVERSA
SCANNO · PENNE

Looking east from the Gianicolo in Rome on a clear day, you can see the hazy purple Apennines of the Abruzzo. With many of the peaks way over 2000 metres high, they create a great natural barrier between Lazio and the Abruzzo, whose other borders are formed by Molise to the south, the Adriatic to the east and The Marches to the north. Nothing in Lazio prepares you for the grandeur and magnificence of the Abruzzo. Neither is there anything in Umbria, The Marches or Tuscany to match the dramatic configuration of the Abruzzo landscape. Some of its most spectacular scenery surrounds the A24 motorway from Rome to Pescara, which every so often meets a sheer wall of rock and so plunges into the mountainside through a tunnel. Higher and higher it climbs above the lands of the ancient Marsi, who may have been descended from the even more ancient race of the Sabines, or perhaps from Marsius, son of Circe, or Marsyas, who was flayed alive for having dared to challenge Apollo.

The motorway skirts the Fucino basin, once a lake where Emperor Claudius staged a huge sham naval battle in which, according to Tacitus, twenty thousand slaves and condemned criminals had to fight each other to the death; now this is the most fertile piece of reclaimed land in the region. Climbing dramatically, effortlessly, the road hugs the contours of the mountains and, as it emerges from the long tunnels, sudden dramatic views of the countryside open up; down below are valleys where there doesn't appear to be a single track, just forest and scrub, or great sweeps of rock and dried up river beds. The only punctuating marks are blobs of buildings, which, on closer inspection, turn out to be hill towns perched high up for their own protection.

Everyone who goes to the Abruzzo remarks on its landscape. A traveller in the late nineteenth century, Anne MacDonell, called it 'the land of peak and pit, of range and gully, red-brown as from the fires of a kindled furnace, full of unquiet shapes and of great silence …'. In some ways I envied these early travellers, who must have experienced ways of life entirely untainted by the modern age. Although MacDonell goes on to say that only

Some of the buildings of Loreto Aprutino (above) have seen better days. Beneath the parish church at Cocullo (right), is a cave where San Domenico Abate, the town's patron saint, once lived as a hermit.

recently the region had been opened up by roads and some incredible 'railroads', she must have seen age-old activities being pursued in the hill townships. Today, the dispersal of the population throughout the rest of the country, and the universality of language and eating habits as a result of the influence of television and travel, have caused the demise of this ancient way of life.

However, another nineteenth-century traveller, the Hon. Keppel Craven, found a land of 'fabulous obscurity'. This still survives in parts, as I found out, if you are prepared to look for it. Astonishingly, there are still towns, only a few kilometres apart, where dialects differ radically, or, as MacDonell found, the people have a lazy nature in one and are industrious in another – towns less than twelve kilometres from one another. Most have very ancient cooking traditions, and in some the inhabitants still wear traditional costumes; the further south you go in Italy, the more common this becomes, until eventually the sight of a female petrol pump attendant in an only marginally updated medieval costume seems quite normal. In others, pagan rituals have survived as a result of their acceptance by the Church; often they are amalgamated with the celebration of some marginal saint's feast day, which serves as a front and provides an excuse for their continuation, making them more acceptable.

The little town of Cocullo is perhaps the most startling of the Abruzzo hill towns. No architectural gem, it is a rough earthbound place, ragged around the edges, poor and very basic. Emerging from the tunnel to the east of the Fucino basin, I couldn't actually see it until, when directed to it via an exit from the motorway, it suddenly loomed up in front of me on a hill beneath two towers, dusty and pale brown. The countryside all around it is ramshackle and full of pits; here and there goats wander about at random among old cars and bamboo. The ground all around is stony and yields very little.

There would be no reason ever to come to Cocullo if it wasn't for the *festa* celebrated there on the first Thursday in May, in honour of the town's patron saint, San Domenico Abate. This festival revolves around one thing only: snakes. San Domenico Abate is only incidental to the occasion, and anyway who can relate to him – wooden, inert, and only dragged out and dusted once a year? Seemingly pagan, various practices associated with this festival were abolished earlier this century by the Church hierarchy, who professed to have had no idea they were going on. But they couldn't ban an entire ceremony that had been practised for nearly 2000 years, and some of the more unusual parts of it remained. Gradually however, stealthily, the other 'lost' bits are creeping back. This event is a manifestation of the natural process of gradual assimilation of pagan ritual into Christian worship, a practice that often went on among the people of primitive Catholic societies. It was a way of uniting pagan and Christian so that they were no longer rivals. Many, many Italian *feste* have their origins in this mixture of influences.

The ancestors of the people of Cocullo, the

The procession wends its way through Cocullo; local girls in traditional costume, carrying circular loaves like huge wheels on their heads, are followed by the statue of San Domenico Abate.

ancient Marsi, who were so abhorrent to the Romans, and so intractable, possessed the power to charm the numerous reptiles said to inhabit their country. By tradition, their descendants 'pretend' to possess the same powers and seem able to charm venomous snakes, rendering them innocuous. Craven said that he once saw a charmer exhibiting his powers: he 'slightly scratched the hand or arm [of a believer] with a viper's tooth divested of its venom; then applied a mysterious stone to the puncture; and finally [furnished] the patient with an image of, and a prayer to, San Domenico di Cocullo …'. This is a good example of what Craven goes on to call 'modern devotion having transferred to a sanctified being the attributes which ancient superstition ascribed to "dealers" in necromancy and divination'.

The 'dealer' in this district originally took the form of Circe's sister Angizia, whose daughters were witches, and who was herself venerated by the Marsi people. Angizia is supposed to have been the goddess of snake charming in the ancient Marsican culture. She held a sort of mystic court in the woods near a town called Luco, which still exists, a few kilometres away, south of Avezzano. Angizia's powers have since been transferred to San Domenico, who was in fact a harmless old hermit who lived in a cave in the mountains, and in another cave which still survives under the sanctuary dedicated to his name in Cocullo. He made friends, St Francis-style, with wild things, and it seems that he was also a snake charmer himself.

A seventeenth-century story tells of the time San Domenico entered the town and the population fell on their knees, begging him to leave them something of his before he departed. The people, most of them shepherds, needed some kind of defence against maladies inflicted by venomous animals, in particular snakes, which populated their countryside; the saint gave them one of his teeth. San Domenico acquired for himself a level of deification that would have surprised even him; he subsequently became patron saint of the town.

Everyone from Cocullo, from the little villages in the Luri valley, and those in the province of Frosinone, another area in which San Domenico was particularly active, and even people from Rome, come to take part in this *festa*. It begins early in the morning with the unruly explosions of fireworks and crackers, after which everyone goes out into the streets and proceeds in single file to San Domenico's sanctuary, singing hymns in praise of the saint. Actually, although San Domenico's cave is still there, the church itself very nearly vanished in the 1981 earthquake, so for the time being the actual focus of the event has been moved to the little, older, church up the hill.

Originally, and until ninety years ago, if you entered the church at this point, two happenings would have surprised you: the faithful would have picked up a handful of soil which had been piled behind the altar, and, with their teeth, would have bitten a cord onto which had been tied a little bell. The soil, taken from the floor of San Domenico's cave and still thought to contain saintly radio-active properties, was

*S*an Domenico Abate, laden with writhing serpents, is carried from his sanctuary, through Cocullo.

for scattering around the houses and fields, and was meant to protect children from death by snakebite. The cord and bell were supposed to protect the villagers from toothache, relieve toothache pain, and prevent anyone bitten by a rabid dog from dying. This second action derived from the fact that, over the centuries, toothache sufferers had believed in kissing San Domenico's tooth – the one he left behind – in order to relieve themselves of the pain. They then tied to the aching tooth a cord, which in turn was attached to a little bell, a kind of 'toothbell', which no doubt was intended to rouse the saint from his slumbers in Paradise. A disapproving bishop banned these practices, but tradition is strong and gradually the villagers are slipping back into their old ways.

Originally the high point of the event would have taken place after the Mass, when the snake catchers, the *serpari*, entered the church with sacks of vipers, grass snakes and other indigenous serpents, and flung them by the handful at the statue. Nowadays this happens outside the church doors, since animals of all kinds are forbidden to enter the building. Some catch hold of the statue's arm, others his neck, and any who fall are quickly replaced. This symbolically exorcizes the serpents, and from that moment they are 'no longer venomous'. The procession then leaves the town, with the snakes slithering all over the painted statue, who stares indifferently ahead, and proceeds to a small valley where more fireworks are let off; there the *festa* continues until the evening, everybody fortified by quantities of raw spirits and coils of bread baked like snakes.

In the front of the procession are the girls of the town, dressed in traditional costume and carrying circular loaves like huge wheels on their heads and in their arms. The *carabinieri* are there in their ceremonial finery, with their Bourbon-style hats on, and there are people in anoraks with video cameras who rush about getting in the way. Others carry large wobbling

The Palazzo Castiglione, just inside Penne's walls, dominates the Porta San Francesco.

dolci (cakes) topped by ears of corn and wild flowers. At one time the snakes were killed at this point, usually at nearby Villalago – more a ritual sacrifice than anything else – but nowadays they are taken back to where they were found, in the belief that they will show up again at the appointed time the following year.

People of all ages grab the snakes, stroking them and pulling at them, and even the priests have them wrapped firmly round their necks and coiled round their wrists as they march along in procession. The old women are dab hands at snatching unsuspecting reptiles. If they do manage to wind one round their necks, and can bear the cold horror of the snake's scaly skin against their own, they will supposedly obtain longevity and never succumb to disease; the snakes are also supposed to render women more fertile. As you wander through Cocullo, down the Via Roma, your progress is monitored from cracks in the shutters of the windows by ancient wrinkled crones who, no doubt, have a lifetime of relationships with snakes behind them.

Cocullo isn't remote compared with the village of Castrovalva, south of Cocullo on the very narrow SS 479. On the other side of a tragic place called Anversa degli Abruzzi, Castrovalva is a kind of eagle's nest, high on the peak of a mountain nearly 1000 metres above the River Sagittario. To get there you have to skirt the narrow ravine on a precipitous road, which alternates between tunnel and terrifying stretches of tarmac, glued to a shelf in the cliff-side. You then branch to the left up an almost vertical slope – very beautiful and no less dramatic – if your car will make it (the locals tend to find donkeys easier), and on through the undergrowth, up and up, with views across to Anversa on one side and to Monte Genzana on the other, until you finally stop in a little open space on the edge of the town.

The hands of the town's clock came to a halt at 3.25 long ago. No one minds. Time has no value up here, where everyone stops dead in their tracks to stare at you as you walk by – everyone meaning all the old women and a few old men. There seem to be more of the former here than the latter; the women sweep the pavements, dig the allotments and push around wheelbarrows full of clods of earth and farm implements while their men sit about on the bench outside the post office and watch.

There isn't much to see here, apart from a couple of ancient chapels, the Chiesa di San Michele (twelfth century) and the Chiesa di Santa Maria (of unspecified date, though most probably as early as the other). There are no shops to buy things in, but Castrovalva is a good example of one of the remoter places that was once a fairly important strategic town, monitoring the comings and goings in the valleys all around it. Nowadays the centre of activity is the post office, to which everyone gravitates at some point in the day.

If you live in Castrovalva, you shop in Anversa, which was once the location of some very curious rituals carried out mostly by the women of the town. Whether or not these still take place here is not revealed, but the women of Anversa used to go on what was called the 'Viaggio di San Giacomo' (the Journey of San

Loreto Aprutino (left) *and the entrance to the Castello Chiola in Loreto Aprutino (above).*

Giacomo). According to De Nino's *Usi e Costumi* (Usage and Custom), barefooted women would meet at four in the morning in the church of San Nicola, each carrying a rosary in one hand and a stick in the other. After a quick prayer on their knees, the first woman tapped the ground with her stick and everyone rose. Silently, and with the same rites, they visited all the churches in the town – San Marcello, with its magnificent gothic portal, Santa Maria delle Grazie, with its sixteenth-century doorway and a rustic fifteenth-century triptych representing St Francis and St Michael, and the church of San Vincenzo. At the church of Our Lady of the Snows, instead of tapping the ground, the women tapped the church door and then went into the building; eventually they left their sticks there and returned home for the night. Nobody offers any explanation for these rites.

Other sinister associations derive from D'Annunzio's *La Fiaccola sotto il Moggio* (The Light under the Bushel), a gothic tragedy of doom and destruction, and from tales describing the complete degeneration of a noble Abruzzese family; these were based on a series of appalling incidents enacted in the castle of Anversa, which today is nothing more than a bit of old derelict wall and a pile of rubble in a farmyard. As the story goes, there was once a

Adverts for wine and cake on a wall in Pescocostanzo (above). (Right) An antique doorway at Loreto Aprutino.

baron of Anversa, a man called Don Titta, who exercised his feudal 'rights' over a neighbour's new wife. Her disapproving husband was removed at a banquet in the castle, and his severed head was served to his wife on a silver dish the same night. The woman's brother-in-law swore revenge and shortly afterwards burned the castle down. This is the reason for its present ruinous state.

In spite of this grisly past, or perhaps because of it, there is a crazed happy-go-lucky air about the place, not helped by the travelling vegetable seller, who parks his van outside the doors of the church in the piazza – the only piazza – selling lettuces and apples to very loud Italian pop music, which emanates from the loudspeakers hidden among the cabbages. Any ghost languishing in a forgotten fissure of this sorry place would have fled by now, pursued by this horrible sound, which fills the air one day every week. My presence, with my Milanese number plates, incited him to turn it up, so I quickly left.

Beyond Villalago, about nine kilometres from Castrovalva, is Scanno; the archetypal tourist town, it has a varied mixture of tenacious ancient traditions and self-conscious customs

which have been revived and packaged for the visitors. It lies in the south-west corner of the region, 1030 metres above sea level, on the very edge of the Parco Nazionale degli Abruzzi, a protected area – open to the public – which still contains bears. Scanno has eighteen hotels which is perhaps a measure of the beauty of the Parco Nazionale and its popularity among tourists.

The *centro storico* itself is untainted by modern development. However, the approach to it from the Lago di Scanno has been fairly extensively developed, and a trail of ribbon development accompanies the road out of the town, still the SS 479, going south towards Villetta Barrea. A walking tour around the old town would begin in the Piazza Santa Maria della Valle, where the old men sit on a circular wooden bench built round an old pine tree in the centre of the piazza. They don't bother to move when it rains. The 360-degree view of the

piazza makes it an excellent vantage point and seating space is consequently at a premium; if anyone gets up their place is immediately taken by another. The buses from the outlying towns stop here, and these same buses will take you through the Abruzzo to convenient stopping points from which to go walking. Here too, opposite the Chiesa Santa Maria della Valle, is the Azienda di Soggiorno e Turismo, where you can get information about and maps of the area.

From the piazza, narrow lanes lead into the *centro storico* which, as in any other hill town, is full of layers of buildings piled on top of one another, some with baroque doorways, others with romanesque or Renaissance ones. In upper windows you catch glimpses of old women embroidering, sitting at the windows to catch the last of the daylight. These women, and some of the younger ones too, still wear a very peculiar dress consisting of a dark green, almost black, skirt made of thick cloth, with a red hem,

*F*uel waiting to be stacked in one of the town's cavernous subterranean basements (above).
The little hill town of Loreto Aprutino is overleaf.

a blue bodice and balloon sleeves; sometimes the whole lot is topped by a blue, brown, purple or green apron. You see them pottering about in the supermarket wearing this outfit, which is undoubtedly warm in winter but they must long for something lighter in summer.

Anne MacDonell visited Scanno and found that the women carried everything on their heads. She doesn't mention the men, who were no doubt sitting in the piazza around the pine tree. The women she saw were carrying loads ranging from a plough to an iron bedstead to huge sacks of grass, all of which, she adds encouragingly, gave them thick necks. While such sights aren't common in Scanno nowadays (and I don't remember having seen any especially thick necks), the women still do a lot of the work in these country areas, not least driving the country bus and handing out parking tickets (wearing tight regulation trousers rather than billowing medieval costume) in the long, straight Strada Roma.

The loop from Scanno to Pescocostanzo by way of Villetta Barrea and Castel di Sangro takes you through varied countryside, a mixture of Arcadian wilderness and rough mountainous scrubland, which is beautiful for its virgin qualities. Only sheep roamed across these hillsides

Santa Maria in Colleromano.

and, in the winter, the shepherds, who were virtually nomads. Their flocks, sometimes numbering thousands, would be driven by huge white wolflike sheepdogs, which you still see today, now much tamer than in the past. With sheep and dogs their only companions, these shepherds amused themselves playing the pipes, and ate rough-and-ready food cooked using wild herbs and vegetables.

It is not surprising therefore that pasta and mutton, lamb and kid form the basis of the region's cooking. In particular, roast *abbacchio*, suckling lamb, is a favourite dish and is invariably delicious. And of course there are the cheeses resulting from an over-abundance of sheep: *scamorza*, made in the mountainous parts of the countryside, which is grilled and then eaten while baking hot; not unlike *mozzarella*, this is a meal in itself. *Caciotta* cheeses are made from ewe's milk, and there is a very particular *pecorino*, which the shepherds make in their mountain cabins. This has an unusually piquant taste and is used for grating. Another variety is *caciocavallo*, so named because two of them are strung together as if astride a horse; this contains a lump of butter which, if you aren't expecting it, is a nasty slippery shock.

Best drunk with these rustic cheeses is a red wine – almost black in fact – called Montepulciano d'Abruzzo, which is of DOC quality. Trebbiano d'Abruzzo, a white wine from Chieti (near Pescara on the coast), is also good with cheese and, if more than a year old, is excellent with fish. The invigorating local wines, the Pergolone, Roseolo and Rustico, won't normally be found outside the Abruzzi. Good basic wines, they are the natural accompaniment to pasta dishes – *maccheroni alla chitarra* being a particular favourite of the region. The *chitarra* is a wooden board with wire strings on which the pasta is cut, and the end result is thick square spaghetti. The sauce served with it is generally made using plain olive oil and *peperoncino*; an ingredient of most of the dishes of the Abruzzo,

these hot red peppers give the food a savoury quality for which it is much revered in Italy. It is said that if the chef in a restaurant comes from the Abruzzo then the food is likely to be very good indeed.

In north-eastern Abruzzo are Penne and Loreto Aprutino, both hill towns of great interest. Penne can be reached from the A25 Avezzano–Pescara route, or from a number of lesser roads from Pescara itself. Whichever way you go, the countryside will be rugged and the roads convoluted and slow. The town stands in a wonderful position, just below the Gran Sasso mountains, whose highest peaks are at nearly 3000 metres. It is a typical rural centre with two interesting early churches, the Duomo and the church of San Giovanni, which is mostly fourteenth century. Almost completely built of tiny bricks, Penne glows orange early in the morning and at dusk appears to be on fire.

From the Porta San Francesco the Via Castiglione winds up through the town, past small provincial *palazzi*, whose grand gestures on a miniature scale give a theatricality to the street scene. The Palazzo Castiglione, opposite the Porta San Francesco, with its tiered balconies and wrought iron, has seen better days, while in the Via Muzio Pansa, the most important street in the town, are some rather more ancient houses, like the medieval Casa dei Vestini. Here also is the fifteenth-century Palazzo del Bono and the Palazzo Tirone, designed by Francesco Dissio.

By the Porta San Francesco is the Dolci Rustici Abruzzesi da Mafalda, a shop selling cakes and sweet pastries. With the AGIP petrol station dumped rather unceremoniously beside it, it seems an unlikely spot in which to find some typical examples of Abruzzese *dolci*, like the *torrone di fichi secchi*, a nougat from nearby Chieti made with dried figs, and *sanguinaccio*, a particularly repellant mixture of freshly killed pig's blood, candied fruit, almonds, nuts and *mosto* – the must from the wine harvest.

SARDINIA

ARITZO · DESULO · ORGOSOLO

Sardinia is enmeshed in a timeless web of its own prehistory, and not surprisingly, perhaps, its people have a startling familiarity with their distant ancestry. All around them, scattered throughout the desolate untouched landscape, are extensive ruins of Nuraghic settlements, some of which date from as early as 1500 BC, remains of the greatest civilization Sardinia ever had. Unique to Sardinia, it was remarkably advanced and, the Romans found, slow to conquer. Some of these ruins are in such a good state of preservation for their age that you can permit yourself an imaginative reconstruction of life at the time. The ruins are a great source of pride to the islanders today.

Ever since the fall of the Nuraghic people, Sardinia has been just another item of booty in imperialist swagbags. Conquerors came and went as they did in Sicily, though the physical evidence of their presence on the island tends to be confined to the odd building on the coast, to dialectal contributions and to variations in regional cooking. The range of buildings constructed by the invaders is limited, consisting mainly of churches, and, unlike Sicily, there was little attempt to assimilate different styles or even cultural patterns in order to formulate something as uniquely Sardinian as the Nuraghic culture clearly was.

The beginning of the end of this highly developed civilization came with the unceasing wars which the Phoenicians, the Carthaginians and then the Romans forced on the Nuraghic tribes. After the first Punic War the Sardinian natives fled to the inaccessible mountains which cover much of eastern Sardinia, an area the Romans came to call Barbaria, from the barbarous valour of the people. Even today this area, now called the Barbagia, around the Monti del Gennargentu, is still relatively isolated. The people who went to live there, whose descendants now occupy the hill towns of Aritzo, Belvi, Desulo, Tonara, Fonni and Orgosolo, developed in isolation from the rest of the island. While the conquerors generally preferred to keep to the coastal areas, the island's geography protected the mountain people, who were free to hang on to their own culture – dialects, costume, traditions and folklore.

Built as high as possible for their own protection, these hill communities turned their backs on the world and the countryside beyond

Away from the main streets, and from the traffic, Desulo (above) is still a primitive, earthbound place. Deeply cavernous shops (right) obscured by darkness keep out the midday sun.

their towns. So contained and secure were they that many of the individual dialects are still in use today—some are very un-Italian. Much of it is unadulterated Latin. If a reincarnated ancient Roman were to visit some of the mountain areas he would have no difficulty in understanding the language. For example, words such as *domus* – house – survive, being preferred to the more usual, and Italian, *casa*. Parts of northern Sardinia retain Spanish in their dialects while other areas, particularly in the north-east, have Tuscan, reflecting the wave of Pisan invaders of the eleventh century. In the south there are traces of Genoese to be heard for exactly the same reason.

Sparsely populated, Sardinia is a fairly primitive land of precipitous valleys alternating with wide, open, barren plains. There is no shortage of routes into the interior, some following the original Roman roads through the river valleys or snaking across the plains; others were built either by Mussolini before the

Second World War or by the Americans after it. Nonetheless, progress by car is very slow. In the Barbagia region, the most mountainous part of the island, the towns are reached via a series of hairpin bends, whose tightly folded coils seem to have lassoed the sides of the mountains. Single track roads are more often than not occupied by cows and sheep, with their jangling bells, than by cars, and in these lonely heights the only living thing on the horizon might be a

lone horseman, a shepherd leaning on his stick contemplating the ground or an eagle sailing with the wind way above.

All the towns of the Barbagia can be reached by blue country bus service from all the provincial capitals; access is easy from either Cagliari or Nuoro. In fact the country bus service is so efficient that the most unexpected connections can be made, usually to suit the convenience of the villagers, shepherds and country people who

use it most. Back roads, gravel roads riddled with potholes, secret roads in dark narrow valleys – nothing impedes the path of the state bus service. And while the main centres of Sardinia are connected by the lines of the state railway, there is a smaller gauge track that spasmodically serves some of the country towns.

Aritzo, on the western slopes of Gennargentu, is one of the main centres in the Barbagia Belvi. The SS 128 runs through the centre of it, changing its name as it does so to Viale Kennedy. On either side, small two-storey houses fall away in orange pantiled terraces down the side of the hill, to the edge of the surrounding woodland. Front doors open directly onto Viale Kennedy, and throughout the day boxes of apricots, plums, peaches and tomatoes languish on the steps; each family sells whatever is superfluous to their needs. From them you can buy tomatoes as huge and as firm

The Nuraghic people were one of the most sophisticated of the early Mediterranean civilizations. Some of their remains (far left) date from as early as 1500 BC. Desulo (above) is a sequence of rough villages joined to form a mountain town with nothing much to recommend it architecturally.

as apples, which people eat raw as they go about their daily business.

The Sardinians in the mountainous regions eat richly scented meat – game, baby lamb or kid – cheese and bread. This simple diet hasn't changed much for centuries, and the Hotel Muvara in Aritzo is a good place to try it. Here suckling pig, lamb and kid are all cooked very simply on the spit or *a carragiu*. This, a traditional Sardinian method of cooking meat, involves digging a deep hole, building a fire at the bottom of it, laying stones over the fire, putting the meat on top of the stones, and then covering the whole lot with myrtle branches overlaid with more stones and earth. The dining

room has a huge fireplace outside its main doors for this purpose. On other occasions wild boar (*cinghiale*) and whole calves are served, each heavily scented with wild herbs, and suckling pig (*porceddu*) is so well cooked here that the chunks of meat literally fall away from the bone.

All around Aritzo are dense woodlands, rich in game and full of holm oaks and chestnuts. In fact so abundant are the chestnuts that each October Aritzo holds a *Sagra delle Castagne* (Feast of the Chestnuts), to which people from all over the island come. Huge smoking braziers are distributed around the town, and the roasted chestnuts are handed around to everyone. This ritual marks the onset of

*M*urals throwing light on obscure political thoughts, enliven the walls of the town of Orgosolo.

autumn, but is really an occasion for standing around gossiping. Another 'nut' festival is the *Sagra delle Nocciole* (Feast of the Hazelnuts), on the fourth Sunday of October. On this occasion a procession in local costume precedes the distribution of hazelnuts and the local nougat called *torrone*.

The Viale Kennedy sweeps past the Hotel Muvara and into Aritzo, skirting on the way a little shaded piazza beside the Bar Castello; here, in the ferocious summer heat, old men and their dogs sit about lethargically in the shade of the heavy old oaks. Further on, the road passes artisans' shops selling rather anaemic ceramics covered in mushroom-coloured splatters, and a shop selling car radios in a very antique setting; finally, at the end of the town, it reaches a tiny market which, having done the round of other neighbouring towns, comes to Aritzo on Fridays. Dusty hollyhocks peer at it over the wall opposite, and the pungent smell of fig leaves does its best to disguise the smells of domestic cleaning equipment and cheap scent on sale. Few country housewives bother to shop in stores. Instead they prefer to wait until the market passes by, when they can stock up at a much cheaper rate.

Apart from the Ethnographic Museum, there isn't much to detain a traveller at Aritzo. Once you've walked past the people waiting for the bus in the Viale Kennedy, all of them, men, women and children, squatting on their haunches in the shade, it is time to take to the hills. Everyone stares at strangers. This is the most unnerving feature of the Sardinian hill towns. My passage through Aritzo was subject to the usual wolf whistles from rather brutish-looking women in black lycra cycling shorts, sitting in groups on the pavement.

Desulo, about eighteen kilometres from Aritzo, and another important centre for touring in the Gennargentu, has some of the most outstandingly distinctive costumes in Sardinia. The women wear scarlet dresses with bands of gold, tight embroidered waistcoats and Dutch-style hats in bright orange, blue and gold. Even in the hottest months of the year they wear this costume, the material of which is generally handwoven at home. Flashes of scarlet can be seen throughout the day as the women go about such arduous tasks as manning the petrol pump, dragging logs to the family store and piling them on the steps or on the roof of the house. It is very often the case that the husbands are itinerant shepherds, away looking after flocks in the Gennargentu.

Desulo is in fact a series of little villages, joined together to form one town. The first is called Asuai, the second Ovolaccio and the third, where the parish church stands, Issiria. Above them, to the east, are two of the highest peaks in Sardinia, Punta la Marmora and the Brancu Spina, while below in the valley are thick woodlands of oak, chestnut and cork oak, the latter curious-looking trees stripped bare of bark from below the first branches.

From Desulo, a narrow country road weaves through the mountains for twenty-four kilometres, over a series of continuous ridges and peaks – not unlike the Alps, only smaller – to Fonni, the highest town in Sardinia, in the Barbagia di Ollolai. On the way, past wild pigs scuffling about beside the road, are little cultivated plateaux and small pastures as well as the odd *baracca*, the little rough stone sheds where the shepherds bivouac while their flocks graze.

Aritzo, Belvi, Desulo, Fonni and Tonara lie in a ring around the Gennargentu. All of them are concerned mainly with sheep rearing, though none of them actually have their own grazing. In November the shepherds herd their charges to the Campidano region, between Cagliari and Oristano, away from the snow, where they remain until May. These itinerant shepherds live on cheeses which they make themselves from sheep's milk – such as *ricotta*, the surplus of which they send back home, and

pecorino, a more mature hard cheese – and game, such as hare, wild boar and *mufloni*, the local wild sheep (although this is now protected by law and it is forbidden to shoot it).

At Fonni there is the *Festa della Beata Vergine dei Martiri*, which is a big Whitsun gathering marking the return of the shepherds after the winter. Lasting from the Thursday to the Sunday after Whitsun, it is a celebration eagerly awaited by the people of the province. A procession takes pilgrims to the local sanctuary, where they stay for a few days in stone huts or in the sanctuary, eating, drinking and reciting prayers. This *festa* is also quite common in other parts of the island and generally it takes the same form. Most people come in their local costumes, whose colours and designs distinguish one town from the next.

Beyond Fonni are Orgosolo and Mamoiada, also in the Barbagia di Ollodai. From Mamoiada to Orgosolo, *carabinieri* activity enlivens the otherwise deserted countryside; jeeps, motorbikes and vans are everywhere. Orgosolo is the focus of incessant friction, with murders and vendettas, claiming the lives of neighbouring families on a regular basis. So quickly and so stealthily does death by murder strike that the *carabinieri* rarely, if ever, find the culprit, although the family feuds which provide the motive are often generations old and fairly common knowledge. Outsiders have nothing to fear; they won't be gunned down on entry, and certainly the people of Orgosolo, once contact has been made, are as friendly and as hospitable as any in Sardinia.

Superficially, Orgosolo is not unlike any other hill town in Sardinia. Unremarkable architecturally, it has a twisting main street, with piles of small, low houses and a few shops wedged into narrow lanes and passages on either side. But there is an intense and explosive atmosphere in this town, which is fuelled by the political murals covering the walls of some of the buildings, and by the resolute, almost

Aritzo is one of the main centres in the sparsely populated Barbagia region around Monti del Gennargentu.

desperate religious intensity of the black-draped women who pour out of the church on Sunday, cowering beneath cowl-like head-scarves drawn up over their mouths. Hugging the walls, they go silently home, fingering the beads of their long black rosaries and looking at the ground. Bawdy, rough young men loll about on windowsills in the main street, trying to pick a fight, throwing accusing stares at passers-by, while old men sit silent and watchful in the shade opposite, observing their movements and shaking their heads.

In August Orgosolo celebrates its *Festa dell'Assunta*, near the ancient sanctuary dedicated to Sant'Anania who, according to tradition, was martyred, along with her companion Sant'Egidio, on the site on which the church now stands. On this occasion the villagers throw their vendettas to the wind and join up in an enormously long procession, which weaves

*F*olk art; a wall painting in Touara.

through the narrow streets of the town behind a statue of the sleeping Virgin, who reclines under a large white net on a sort of funerary bier carried by four men in white 'cassocks'. Young women lead the way, dressed in vivid local costume, the treasured kind made of rich brocades that are passed down from mother to daughter for generations. So important and so revered are the costumes of these communities that even the headscarf worn by the women of Orgosolo is often woven with gold thread.

The bulk of the procession is made up of two streams of older women dressed in black, crow-like, who move stealthily behind the Virgin, their hands tightly clasped around their rosaries. Their heads are covered and their eyes are sunken into furrowed medieval faces. There are no traffic sounds. The only noise is the rhythmic crunch of feet on the gravel road and a dull murmuring in unison of the *festa* prayers.

The old women such as this one (top), *more used to being shut away indoors all day, gravitate to the windows and balconies above the main streets when a stranger passes by. Filling containers at the communal tap* (below)*; this villager sticks to Desulo's traditional form of dress.*

TUSCANY

POPPI · PORCIANO · CORTONA · GARGONZA
MONTEPULCIANO · MONTALCINO

The Tuscan countryside is packed full of hill towns. From one end of the region to the other, scattered over the Garfagnana in the north, the Pratomagno in the north-east, the Colline Metallifere in the west, Chianti and the edges of the Val di Chiana in the east, ancient provincial centres gaze over the countryside from on high. Some are very well known while others are hardly visited, shut away from the mainstream of Tuscan life.

Most visitors to Tuscany know San Gimignano, in the west, a town with thirteen medieval towers – once there were nearly eighty – crammed on a hill within three concentric rings of walls. Less well known is Poppi, in the north-east, balanced on the edge of a ridge way above the field of Campaldino, where the Florentine Guelphs scored a decisive victory over the Aretine Ghibellines in the thirteenth century. Sorano, in the south, well off the beaten track, is a remote, weary place on a table-like crust of rock, full of broken and nearly broken buildings. This town, where the houses of a bludgeoned population lie beside the palace of the ferocious Orsini family, is more typical of nearby Lazio than of Tuscany.

In these and numerous other Tuscan hill towns, the aggressive attitudes and belligerent rivalries of past centuries have been replaced by fierce competition in the production of wine and olive oil. Gone is the raw, watchful defensiveness that dictated the outlook of nearly all these places for so long. Only physical relics of their warlike pasts remain, most striking among them their crenellated walls, ancient brick towers, fortresses and huge city gates.

Tuscany has essentially been 'discovered'. For at least two centuries it has been hallowed ground for disaffected foreign nationals, who have come to renew their spirits in front of the Madonnas and the cycles of frescoes in the apses of the local churches, and to steep themselves in a cultural renaissance that was the most fruitful and the most far-reaching in Italy.

In the fourteenth and fifteenth centuries the cities and hill towns of the region were the scene of the rebirth of the Sciences, Literature, Art and the Humanities, the blooming of a modern enlightened age after the fog of the Middle Ages. Today, an association with the manifestations of the Renaissance – paintings, sculpture, architecture – is the lot of many

San Gimignano's characteristic stone towers (above)*; an antique carved lion keeps guard in Pitigliano* (right).

Tuscan hill towns, and even small country museums are crammed with artefacts representative of the achievements of their own particular locations.

Travellers, writers, idlers, dilettantes and artists from all over Europe have been extolling the virtues of Tuscany for centuries. Shelley regarded Tuscany as the 'paradise of exiles', while Dr Johnson was conscious of a certain sense of inferiority that went with not having been there. Nowadays Chianti, the area between Florence, Siena and Arezzo, is

swamped by the English creating their own version of the Garden of Eden, Tuscan style, which, with the local wine, olive oil and hearty rustic cooking, isn't so difficult.

The obvious attractions of Tuscany are well documented and much visited. Even a remote place like Monterchi, a small, uninteresting little town about seventeen kilometres east of Arezzo, on the Umbrian border, is a mecca for visitors. They come to gaze at Piero della Francesca's *Madonna del Parto* on the wall of a little funerary chapel just outside the town. This is one of the most enchanting and mysterious images of the Renaissance, and they come not to revere her as the Mother of God but to pay homage to the artistic achievements of the pain-

ter who created her in the fifteenth century. A well-trodden path leads down an avenue of cypresses from the little hill town to the graveyard; yet without Piero, nobody would come here and Monterchi would be just another pretty little place on the road to Arezzo (get there by 12.00 p.m. or the chapel will be closed for the afternoon, which will almost certainly mean a wasted journey).

North of Arezzo, if you take the SS 71, are Bibbiena, Poppi, Pratovecchio and Stia, small hill towns whose attractions are less obvious. They lie on the edge of the Pratomagno ridge, in the Casentino, the uppermost stretch of the valley of the River Arno, which flows from its source on Monte Falterone down through Florence to the sea. Apart from the intrinsic beauty of their manmade forms – their silhouettes, crenellations, towers, regular brickwork and stone carving – and their adaptation to the contours of the landscape, they may just have a good wine to taste, or a remarkable view to contemplate.

The views from Poppi, just six kilometres from the market town of Bibbiena, are remarkable. If you stand with your back to its *castello*, sometimes called the Palazzo Pretorio, and look east, you can see in the distance the village of Caprese Michelangelo, Michelangelo's birthplace, among the rocks and boulders high above the upper reaches of the Tiber. Looking the other way, you can see along the rough uneven valley to Romena and the town of Stia beyond, and to the castle of Porciano still further to the north.

In the medieval period Poppi was the centre of the territories of the Conti Guidi. In fact, even before the advent of the Middle Ages, it had been something of a mountain eyrie, from which the tyrannical local barons would swoop down on their defenceless peasants below and brutally disrupt their lives. The traces of their rule here, and right across the Casentino, are very much in evidence today, even though the

The best place to drink a glass of Brunello di Montalcino in Montalcino.

last of them effectively ran out of power in the days of the Renaissance. The chronicles of the period are full of their deeds and misdeeds as one Guidi succeeded another, each one adding to the power and influence of their house and each one more horrendous than the last. The pages of Dante and Giovanni Villani are full of references to the Guidi, and even Buoncompagno, a thirteenth-century grammarian, brims over with details of their appalling behaviour.

One well-known story concerns a delinquent called Guidoguerra IV, who played practical jokes on his courtiers. Punning on the names of three of them – Malanotte, Maldecorpo and Abbas – he once compelled the first to spend the night in the snow on the roof of the castle, the second to lie between two fires so that his extremities were singed and the third to have his hair pulled out in order to simulate a tonsure.

These charming pranks were carried out in the castle at Poppi, a formidable edifice which stands on a rise above the town. It can be seen for miles around: blocklike, with a single tower and a moat, it is a grim reminder of the power and opulence of its builders. The present form

of the castle is largely the result of its rebuilding after the Battle of Campaldino, possibly by Arnolfo di Cambio, who built the Palazzo Vecchio in Florence, a building not dissimilar to this. Today you can visit Poppi's castle, and see the magnificent staircase that leads from the inner courtyard up to the great chambers, one of which contains an important library (consisting of illuminated manuscripts and early books) which originally came from the monks at the nearby monastery of Camaldoli. The castle is also the scene of art and history exhibitions, held every year in July and August.

The castle towers above the site of the Battle of Campaldino, where in 1289 the Guelphs and the Ghibellines tried to settle their differences in a gruesome display of blood-letting and butchery. The single most important monument to this event, apart from a column marking the battle site, is the fifth Canto of Dante's *Divine Comedy: Purgatory* (the young Dante was in the front line fighting for the Florentine Guelphs) where some of the violence, and the sadness, of the event is expressed in the passage dealing with the mortally wounded Guido da Montefeltro, the leader of the Ghibellines, who dragged himself away from the battle scene 'pierced in the throat ...', '... bloodying the plain ...' on his way to die. His body was never found.

The vigour of Poppi's early years has vanished. Although it is the central visual focus

The walls of Montalcino (left) *date from the thirteenth century.* (Above) *Dante looks out over the Casentino from the ramparts of Poppi.*

of this part of the Casentino, it is now a quiet placid place where nothing much happens. The Via Conti Guidi leads up to the castle from the town's main street, the Via Cavour. It then branches to the right, to a small piazza with the town's major restaurant (it is also a *pensione*), the Casentino, a popular venue for Florentine day-trippers who want to sample some of the season's game, in particular *cinghiale* (wild boar). This establishment occupies the site of another Guidi palace, of which nothing now remains apart from a ruinous bit of the old Devil's Tower.

In the Middle Ages this tower was lived in by a particularly barbaric temptress, a Guidi, called Contessa Telda, who used to lure handsome young men into her bed and then fling them through a trap door in the floor to the dungeons below when she'd had enough of them. One day she went too far, luring into her clutches an especially favoured son of a local family. The enraged population of Poppi turned on her, grabbed her unceremoniously, bundled her into the tower and left her there until she eventually starved to death.

The town is laid out on a narrow ridge below the castle. Its central artery, the Via Cavour, has a solid gravity about it; nearly everything is made of stone, and the houses lining it are low and heavy. The pavements on either side are arcaded, and the ribs of the vaulted ceiling above rest on stout piers decorated with a variety of little carved capitals. The arcades are cavernous and dark; your footsteps echo in the shadows against the old walls, and cats scuttle away as you pass. Cut into the wall, or freestanding with scroll-like legs, are little stone benches where a few old men sit and gossip at intervals throughout the day. To either side of the covered pavements are steep flights of steps that disappear into other parts of the town, lower down the ridge.

At one end of the Via Cavour is a quiet, dark parish church of great antiquity, while at the

The Palazzo Pretorio at Poppi dominates the plain of Campaldino, at the battle of which Dante fought for the Florentine Guelphs.

other end, in the Piazza Antonio Gramsci, in front of the town gate, is the local bar. This is, as usual, the meeting point for the town's younger population, which doesn't amount to very much. They operate the fruit machines while the older generation sit idly around them, silently smoking. Sitting here, looking down the empty streets, you are overwhelmed by the air of melancholy, even on a bright, hot day. The town is well kept and the geraniums well watered and neat in their pots, but where are the inhabitants? It could be a ghost town.

Glowering at Poppi from just a few kilometres away are the remains of the eleventh-century Castello di Romena. This enchanting old wreck sits on the hill of Romena, which slopes gently down to the cornfields around Poppi. From wherever you are in the valley you can see Romena and the remains of its towers sticking up into the air. Surrounded by crumbling walls and rampant undergrowth, this is one of the lost *borghi*, medieval villages, of Tuscany. The whole of this hilltop was once encircled by a wall more than half a mile long, which, in Romena's heyday, protected hundreds of local families in times of crisis.

Dante stayed here; Dante seems to have stayed everywhere in this region. One rather suspects that a certain amount of gratuitous prestige is added to a property if the name of the poet can be incorporated somewhere along the line, just as the English and Americans like to claim that Elizabeth I or George Washington once slept in this bed or that. It means that you look at an old ruin with renewed interest, or discover a sudden morbid fascination for an old and otherwise worthless piece of furniture.

A visit to the Romena hilltop after lunch is to be recommended; you can wander off down the path below the castle to the ancient Fonte Branda, drink from the trickle of water from which no doubt Dante quenched his thirst, and retire to sleep among the wild berries and the olives on the derelict grassy terraces. Nearby is the *pieve*, possibly the most important romanesque parish church in the Casentino, built by Countess Matilda. It stands on the edge of the woods and ploughed fields, a setting that cannot have changed much over the centuries. If the building is locked, ask for the key at the adjacent farmhouse, and a very obliging woman will show you around.

From Romena continue towards Stia, a little agricultural town that has arcaded Poppi-like streets, and then on to Porciano, a hamlet just to the north which, once again, Dante visited. Higher than Poppi, it isn't surprising that this place has had the title of Terrazza del Casentino conferred on it. Sit with the lizards on a concrete embankment below the castle in the sun, and admire the view which stretches out to Caprese Michelangelo.

Porciano is dominated by the remains of yet another Guidi castle, though only a single tower of it remains. The Conti Guidi of Porciano once terrorized the neighbourhood, in particular Stia, which they held in a state of terrified subjection for long periods at a time. This seems strange today, now that Porciano has been reduced to a handful of cottages and a scrap of castle that refused to collapse when the rest of it did, and Stia is a large thriving community. Just reward: the Counts of Porciano were hated, and in the *Divine Comedy* Dante likens them to swine. Needless to say, Dante had a look in at Porciano as well – as prisoner, it is thought, and not as guest. The fact that he likened his hosts to *porci* (pigs), in a clever and malicious play on words, may have been what led the Guidi to dump him behind bars, providing hospitality for him in their dungeons in an effort to silence him for a while.

The Casentino is an area of enormous interest. To see it comfortably, it would be best to stay either in Arezzo, a fairly large, interesting town, connected by rail to Florence, eighty-one kilometres away to the north-west, or alternatively at Cortona, about twenty-five

kilometres south of Arezzo. There are some small hotels in this little town, which is poised way above the wide flat plain of the Val di Chiana. Local convents also provide rooms, though they are somewhat austere. Enquire at the local tourist office situated in the Via Nazionale for details.

You could spend a week at Cortona and still not have fully explored the town. It is almost totally enclosed by its walls, and the integrity of its ancient character is remarkable. Perhaps its position is responsible. It lies 650 metres up, on one side of Monte Egidio, and the views to the plain, edged in the blue distance by the mountains enclosing Siena, and to Lake Trasimeno, are among the most extensive from any hill town in Italy.

Access to Cortona is via a dizzy winding road that climbs up among the ilexes, the terraced olive groves and the long dry-stone walls. Up here in the clouds temperatures are perceptibly lower than down in the valley, and in the winter conditions are positively arctic. This is one of Cortona's hidden attributes, though, because it means that it is a very comfortable place to stay in the summer; it is also free from mosquitos, which tend to choose their victims from among the residents of the plain, in particular those around Lake Trasimeno, nine kilometres away.

Cortona is typically medieval in appearance. Supposedly one of the oldest inhabited sites in Tuscany, it was occupied by an early Umbrian tribe even before the Etruscans colonized it. It was the Etruscans who built the city walls and the Porta Colonia at the end of the Via Dardano, and while only bits of their walls survive, the Porta Colonia is still very much in use. The town was later occupied by the Romans; the Aretines (inhabitants of Arezzo) sacked it in 1258 and in 1409 it was sold to the Florentines, thus linking it to the fortunes of the Grand Duchy of Tuscany.

Fiat 500s (above) *are practically the only cars able to negotiate Cortona's narrow ancient alleys and passages. Cortona* (overleaf) *is poised way above the wide flat plain of the Val di Chiana.*

Beyond the church of Santa Maria della Grazia, a kind of halfway point on the slope up to the town, is the Porta Sant'Agostino; this gate lies at the bottom of the Via Guelfa, which leads to Cortona's centre, the Piazza della Repubblica. You can't easily park your car in the town, but because it is so small it is easy to get around without it. Having said that, the steep steps and streets are breathtakingly arduous to climb, and even my reasonably fit calf muscles groaned in agony at the thought of yet another near vertical incline. Why is it that the most interesting little chapels are always at the top of the town?

In the Piazza della Repubblica is the Palazzo Comunale, with its steep flight of steps overlooking the piazza. Here people sit at dusk and watch the crowds milling about during the *passeggiata*.

Just around the corner, overlooking the Piazza Signorelli, is the thirteenth-century Palazzo Pretorio (also known as the Palazzo Casali) which houses the Etruscan Museum. It also contains works of art from local churches – works by Luca Signorelli (who was born in Cortona) and Neri di Bicci. However, it is the Museo Diocesano in the Piazza Duomo, opposite the Duomo, that has the town's greatest masterpieces. There is a School of Duccio *Madonna and Child*, and works by Fra Angelico and Pietro Lorenzetti as well as others by Luca Signorelli. To get there, continue past the Palazzo Pretorio and the cavernous antique shops – of which there are a great many since Cortona hosts a large annual antiques fair in September/October – past the *mercato dell'usato*, the second-hand emporium, which does a roaring trade in old boots and cracked tea cups, usually in tandem with the fair, and on to the Teatro Signorelli; beyond it is the Duomo.

If you can't be bothered to wade through Cortona's artistic heritage, just visit the little church of San Niccolò, which contains one of Signorelli's greatest works, *The Deposition*. As you enter, an ancient person will emerge from the shadows, take your 1000 lire, and then, when you have contemplated the painting, turn it round so that you can see the other side of it: Signorelli's *Madonna and Child with SS. Peter and Paul*. The church itself is something of a curiosity. Tiny and difficult to find, it languishes in a little enclosed courtyard, whose outer walls are surmounted by a single row of cypresses. The immensely steep, practically vertical, Via San Niccolò leads up to it by means of a series of convolutions, steep, shallow steps and slippery pavements. A visit is well worth every ache of your calf muscles, but don't arrive after midday or it will be closed, and nothing will rouse the ancient keeper from her lunch.

Cortona is a lively little town. At the end of the day the older residents cram into the Piazza della Repubblica, which is a small triangular space, and into the even smaller streets opening off it. A wander down towards the Piazza del Duomo always ends with a cigarette break, leaning over the parapet outside the Duomo to watch the sun set over the plain. Below, the countryside falls away in terraces, past the cemetery – which looks not unlike a small town, with its rows of family sepulchres and its little gardens enclosed by a high defensive wall (a

The ubiquitous blue country buses, after creaking and grinding nearly to the summit of Cortona's Monte Egidio, stop for a breather.

common sight in Italy) – past the lines of cypresses and the layers of olive trees and the country villas, until, in the purplish blue distance, you can just make out the Castello di Montecchio Vesponi, which crowns a peak above the main road to Arezzo. A quick look in the Duomo, which isn't very interesting, then back to the Piazza dell Repubblica via the side alleys (with tiny Fiat 500s crammed into every available corner) and eventually to the busier Via Roma.

The *giovanotti* of Cortona, the under twenty-fives, tend to hang about in the Piazza Garibaldi under the marble bust of King Umberto I, a foolish-looking creature sporting, somewhat absurdly, a large walrus moustache. Some loutish creatures lounge about in a curious little bar built under the road; there, behind the thick overhanging vines, they sit and ogle Cortona's female population, waddling by in padded-shouldered T-shirts. Many idle and listless out-

of-school hours are spent here, puffing on MS cigarettes, eating ice creams and listening to the noisy jukebox.

The main streets in the centre of Cortona are lined with shops and bars, and there are a good many restaurants and *trattorie* lurking down the flights of steps, which vanish into the shadows and the warren-like inner recesses of the town. In the Via Dardano is the Trattoria Dardano, which has a great range of *cucina casalinga* (home cooking), Tuscan style. This is often the simplest, perhaps even the most sober, cooking in the whole of Italy: the main ingredients are always olive oil, sage, rosemary, basil and wine, and the results are generally hearty and rustic. Tuscan food hardly lends itself to being prepared on electric stoves or gas cookers; instead, the best dishes are frequently those grilled over chestnut and vine embers on an open fire. Even the plates and bowls you eat off tend to be great earthenware platters or deep

Beyond Montalcino are the vast stretches of pale clay countryside dotted with cypresses and huge squat sixteenth-century villas and farmhouses.

dishes, which are a measure of the seriousness with which Tuscans regard their food. In the Trattoria Dardano, as elsewhere, it's not so much what you choose from the range of possibilities on the menu as how it is prepared. Strangers entering Tuscan restaurants are often surprised to find customers carefully watching slabs of meat on the grill or a small chicken on the spit, for it is they who decide when a meal is ready and not the cook.

Fairly typical as an *antipasto*, and extremely good, are *crostini*, which are little squares of toast laden with paté made from liver and spleen. There might be *fagiolo all'olio*, boiled beans served hot or cold and drenched in olive oil, or *fiori fritti*, courgette (zucchini) flowers fried in batter. The main dishes tend to be slightly heavier, like roast lamb, skewered snipe, hare or rabbit.

About twenty-five kilometres from Cortona as the crow flies, and a great deal further by Fiat, is the little *borgo* of Gargonza, just outside Monte San Savino. More of a castle really, whose walls contain a perfectly preserved thirteenth-century village, Gargonza dominates the Val di Chiana from the centre of its own vast wooded estate. It is still the property of the Guicciardini Corsi Salviati family, whose ancestors were (according to Dante's biographer Leonardo Bruni) Dante's hosts. The poet is thought to have been here in 1304, when the castle was used as a gathering point for Ghibellines from Arezzo and Florence. All of the tiny cell-like former peasants' houses have now been turned into self-catering retreats, simply furnished and efficiently run. Tiny stone streets, a minute rustic chapel dedicated to saints Tiburzio and Susanna, a massive baronial tower – for the use of which the owners had to pay duty to Monte San Savino – peaceful gardens, and a magnificent view through the pines down to the valley below, make Gargonza a very pleasant place to stay.

South of Cortona, a small road leads across

the Val di Chiana to Montepulciano and Chianciano (near the spa town of Chianciano Terme). Although these two towns are very popular, visited mostly by Italians, other little hill towns like Pienza, San Quirico d'Orcia and Montalcino, a few hairpin bends west of Montepulciano, are less frequented except perhaps by wine fanatics in search of the wine called Brunello di Montalcino. This whole region south of Siena is made up of vast stretches of pale clay hillside, each hill's brow fringed with a row of cypresses. Huge old farmhouses, sixteenth-century villas built of orange brick, and old castles litter the landscape.

Montepulciano is the biggest town in this region, sitting 605 metres above sea level, on a hill which dominates the Chianti and Orcia valleys. It lies halfway between Florence and Rome, on the Autostrada del Sole, but you can also get there by train. You have to alight at Chiusi-Chianciano Terme station; then there are buses to Montepulciano which connect with the daily train arrivals.

It suited the Romans to live on this site, the Mons Politianum, though according to a local tale they weren't its first occupants. The town is supposed to have been founded by the legendary Lars Porsena, the Etruscan King of Chiusi, and to support this theory are the many Etruscan artefacts that have been found over the years in the surrounding countryside. The

*O*ld men (left) *sit out the hours of the* dopopranzo *in the shade near the hot dusty piazza in Pitigliano. Wine fanatics (above) are the latter-day plague of Montalcino, famous for its Brunello di Montalcino wine. How to quench your thirst and to still your hunger here is not a problem.*

following centuries are laden with stories of war and bitter rivalry between local noble families and of battles with Florence and Siena. In the Middle Ages, and during the Renaissance, Montepulciano was a wealthy agricultural town, which was much coveted by its neighbouring power-hungry city states. It is from these years that present-day Montepulciano derives its character. The town's economy is still based on the produce of the neighbouring fertile fields and, luckily, twentieth-century industrialization has made no impact here; as a result, Montepulciano, which is full of interesting churches and other buildings, is one of the best-preserved Renaissance towns in Italy.

There are two parts to it. If you are not a very diligent sightseer and are easily phased by steep streets, you'll miss the upper half of the town. It will be your loss and, like Henry James, who was too drunk to sightsee adequately at Montepulciano, you will miss some of the great

works of the early Renaissance. Those shrouded in the gloom of the Duomo are the most important – works by Taddeo di Bartolo, for example, and others by Benedetto da Maiano and Tino da Camaino. There are works by Lorenzo di Credi and Giovanni d'Agostino inside the church of Sant'Agostino, with its façade by Michelozzo, and in Santa Maria dei Servi is a *Madonna and Child* of the school of Duccio. In the church of Santa Lucia is a *Madonna della Misericordia* by Luca Signorelli, and there are loads of other well-known paintings in the Civic Museum, which is housed in the Palazzo Neri-Orselli in the Piazza Grande. Here also is the local Etruscan collection.

The lower town, which connects directly with the road to Chianciano Terme, really starts with the Porta al Prato, at the bottom of the long winding Corso which eventually leads up to the summit of the town. On the way it passes a succession of *trattorie* and shops selling Mon-

The Cantina Brunello, Montalcino.

tepulciano's extra virgin olive oil in great glass flasks and green and gold tins, and local wine and cheese. It also passes some of the town's less interesting buildings, though one of them, a heavily rusticated *palazzo*, now the Banca Popolare dell'Etruria, has a sign above its door saying that Garibaldi was here in 1867. Garibaldi, like Dante, stayed everywhere, and it is a distinct mark of esteem even now to be able to say that he was given hospitality in a particular house – though he probably spent much of his stay in bed with his host's daughter or wife (his host may not of course have been party to knowledge of these events).

Further up the hill the houses become steadily more antique. The road seems to lead out of town for a short while, to a sort of belvedere which looks out over the countryside, then it branches sharply to the right, past the Cantina Gattavecchia, a wine cellar with off sales, and continues climbing back into the town again. The houses near the top of the Corso date mostly from the thirteenth and fourteenth centuries. Eventually, after an arduous climb, you reach the Piazza Grande, and here, like elements in a vast stage set, are the late fourteenth-century Palazzo Comunale and the sixteenth-century Duomo, whose time-worn, scarred façade has been left unfinished.

The steps of the Duomo are the scene of the grand finale of the *Bravio delle Botti*, a barrel-pushing race that takes place in August each year. This involves eight teams, each pushing a barrel weighing 80 kg through the town, up the hill from Sant'Agnese to the Piazza Grande. The teams are called the *contradaioli* and are made up of representatives of the *contrade*, the eight autonomous quarters of the city. Before the race these hefty locals, dressed in fourteenth-century costume, lead a procession through the streets, mapping out their intended route. The race is flamboyant and riotous, and once it is over a great banquet takes place in the streets around the piazza. Everyone joins in.

About the same time a kind of baccanale takes place, which is intended to celebrate that year's Vino Nobile, a local wine (Vino Nobile di Montepulciano) renowned for its excellence. Its name most probably derives from the fact that it was only ever drunk by the district nobility who, spurred on by Francesco Redi's praise for the wine in the seventeenth century – 'of all wines, Montepulciano is king' – drank nothing else. This wine is still one of the champions of the Italian reds, and its status is confirmed by the fact that it is a DOCG wine (*Denominazione di Origine Controllata e Garantita*, name of origin controlled and guaranteed).

Another great Tuscan wine of DOCG status is Brunello di Montalcino, from the town of Montalcino, forty kilometres to the west of Montepulciano. The destiny of this little hill town was linked to Siena's until the end of the fifteenth century when, as the last free commune in Italy, it was taken over by the Grand Duke of Tuscany, Cosimo I. Cut off from the main routes of southern Tuscany, its community has always depended for its livelihood on grapes and olives, in particular the former. From the local grapes comes the delicate white Moscadelletto di Montalcino, which for centuries was drunk with the final course at local banquets. Chilled, and usually served with sweet puddings, it was consumed in vast quantities. You can still get it here, though the popularity of the red Brunello (which is actually slightly brown) has nearly caused its disappearance.

One good place to taste the Brunello, as well as other local estate wines, which you probably won't find in shops elsewhere, is in the castle, the Rocca, at the top of Montalcino. Here there is a small *enoteca* (a vintage wine store), where you can have a simple lunch of bread, salami and cheese. From this *enoteca*, and from others around the town, you can buy guides to the various local wine estates that can be visited and from which, in some cases, wine can be bought.

UMBRIA

PERUGIA · GUBBIO · ASSISI · SPELLO
MONTEFALCO · TODI

Umbria has a fairly unruly landscape, roughened by the undulating foothills and the steep upland valleys of the Apennines, landlocked in the centre of the Italian peninsula. The Umbrians like to think of their country as the 'Green Heart of Italy', a magical, verdant region enclosed on one side by the Tiber valley and on the other by the steep hills along the western edge of The Marches.

Umbria is best observed from the ramparts of some ancient terracotta-coloured hill town or village, a whole range of which crowd its hills. Alternatively you can view the countryside in the paintings of the Umbrian School, in the works of Piero della Francesca, Perugino or Pinturicchio, in which its gentle hills, splattered with soft, translucent light, form the backgrounds to religious works of the Madonna and the saints. Calm, mystical even, these paintings reflect a meditative, almost spiritual landscape. Not much has changed today in Umbria, where St Francis of Assisi once perceived most acutely the work of the Creator. The benign countryside all around him, overlooked by the early fortified hill towns, provided an ideal spiritual retreat, and attracted, among others, St Clare and St Valentine.

But there was nothing mystical about Umbria in the centuries before St Francis. The raw realities of life then forced the inhabitants to retreat to the hilltops for their own protection against warring and aggressive neighbouring tribes. In the days of the early Italic Umbrians (the tribe that eventually gave the region its name) the valleys of central Umbria were lakes. The earliest villages therefore had to be built on high. In time, however, these lakes and marshes dried up, or were drained by the Romans. Nowadays, early autumn mornings suggest what the landscape must have looked like then, with the dawn mist hanging over the valleys like the still, murky waters of the ancient lakes, revealing only the highest peaks, which stick out like the islands of antiquity.

The hill towns overlooking these valleys are among the most evocative in the whole of Italy. They straddle the contours of the hillsides today, remote, medieval and romantic. Perugia, at the head of the Tiber valley, which cuts the region into two parts, is halfway between Città

The Basilica of San Francesco (above), *the Lower Church.*
Assisi (right) *is stretched along the side of Monte Subiaso.*

di Castello in the north and Spoleto in the south. In between are Assisi, Spello, Trevi and Montefalco, and to the west Todi and Orvieto. To the north-east is Gubbio and, further east still, Gualdo Tadino and Nocera. When the Goths invaded Italy after the collapse of the Roman Empire, the Umbrians took to these hilltop crags once again and built stout walls over natural defences, descending into the valleys only to meet and fight their aggressors.

Each of these hill towns was once an autonomous city state, which either terrorized its neighbours or was smitten by internal fighting. The people of Assisi, Spoleto and Gubbio whiled away the centuries fighting off the predatory Perugians, the grimmest and most powerful of all, who regularly launched attacks on all cities within a fifty-mile radius. How the citizens of Assisi must have hated the Perugians, whose capricious, glowering city, crammed onto the top of a steep hill, could be seen about twenty kilometres away. The difference between these two cities at the time is exemplified now by the fact that, in the thirteenth century, the Perugians were great followers of the *battuti*, a strange fraternity of friars whose hysterical excesses, which included self-flagellation, suited the Perugians' volatile temperament, while the Assisans preferred the deeper

Umbrian tradition of mysticism, which flowered in their town under St Francis. This saint didn't appeal to the Perugians. Not only was he Assisan but his gentle message had no place within their rough, inhospitable walls. The Perugians were bred to intemperate violence and, even if they did covet his body after his death, it was only out of antipathy towards their neighbouring city.

Until about thirty years ago Perugia was a typical, sleepy Umbrian city, all fading frescoes, crumbling buildings and sunlit vistas. In 1786 Goethe was enamoured of its 'beautiful situation', finding the view of the lake (Trasimeno, to the west) 'charming'. While the *centro storico* today is much as it was when Goethe walked its streets, he would be hard pressed to express his perceptions of the views of the city from the plain. Surrounded by motorways, Perugia stands at the crossroads between the eastern Umbrian cities and Arezzo and Florence in the north, and its outskirts are not what they were. In between the motorways and the *tangenziale* (the by-pass) are new suburbs, and the factories which provide the nation with some of its pasta.

But its height, at 450 metres, allows the old city to rise above the twentieth century. Happily, it is as inaccessible to the industrial sprawl today as it was to its aggressors in its warring past. There are three main routes into town: from the west, the Via XX Settembre winds up to the centre, through the Porta Eburnea and eventually to the Piazza Italia; from the east, the Via XIV Settembre struggles up to and under the Porta Santa Margherita and into the Piazza IV Novembre, the city's most beautiful square; and the Corso Cavour enters the city through the Porta San Pietro. Don't even think of taking your car into the centre; after 8.00 a.m. you can't get in at all because the narrow streets cannot accommodate traffic, and the *polizia stradale* (the street police) will almost certainly turn you away. Park below, in one of the many car parks built especially for this purpose, or

A detail of the Fontana Maggiore in Perugia's central Piazza IV Novembre.

else just squeeze into any available gap by the roadside, like everyone else.

Perugia, within its ramparts, beyond its massive gateways, is still the martial face of Umbria. Streets of fortified palaces and gaunt, crenellated civic buildings march towards the Piazza IV Novembre and its medieval Duomo. In the past the Perugians were often aggressive for its own sake and with an inconstancy which was bewildering. Not only were they one of the most belligerent partisans of the Guelph (papal) cause in Umbria but they also spent much of their history engaged in acts of defiance against the Pope in Rome. They terrorized neighbouring city states, and individual noble families fed off excessively bloodthirsty disputes, slaughtering their opponents *en masse* or killing off their own members in bitter infighting.

The Baglioni family were the worst offenders. In the middle of the sixteenth century, when one of them murdered the papal legate, Pope Paul III dispatched his troops to Perugia to crush the clan and their followers. He then went so far as to demolish their palaces and other houses in Via Baglioni and to construct a massive fortress called the Rocca Paolina in their place. This was meant as a final act of retribution for their crimes. With Sangallo as architect, this fortress rose from the rubble of over four hundred houses and no less than ten churches.

Today you can descend, through to an Etruscan gate, the Porta Marzia, to a subterranean Via Baglioni beneath Piazza Italia, and shiver with the ghosts of the Baglioni murderers in the gloom of the remains of some of their palaces; by some strange accident, parts of them survived intact beneath the Rocca Paolina. Perhaps the papal authorities used them as dungeons. The Baglioni clan had the last laugh, however. In 1848 the Perugians began smashing to bits this symbol of hated papal authority; so massive was it that only thirty years later was most of its bulk removed. The Via Baglioni was

opened up in part, and today it forms an access route from lower Perugia to the Piazza Italia. The passages are still roofed over and, in a sublime juxtaposition of ancient and modern, an escalator rises from the gloom, past the blocked-up windows of Grifone Baglioni's tower, taking office workers to their jobs.

The Corso Vanucci (named after the painter Perugino, whose real name was Pietro Vannucci) meets the Piazza IV Novembre beside the Palazzo dei Priori. Between this building, Perugia's Civic Centre since the end of the thirteenth century, which dominates the Corso, and the Duomo opposite, is the Fontana Maggiore, one of Italy's most spectacular fountains. It is also one of the great works of early Italian artistic achievement: constructed in three tiers, like a huge marble cake, it was sculpted in 1277 by Nicola and Giovanni Pisano, father and son; their work, both as individual artists and as a team, is scattered about between the Baptistry at Pisa, Siena Cathedral and Pistoia.

I wonder how many of the Perugians who mooch about in the piazza today, or loll against the spiked fence encircling the fountain, joking, laughing and talking, ever remember that here in the piazza, in the Middle Ages, their ancestors slaughtered one another mercilessly in senseless faction fighting on more than one

*P*erugia is in many ways still a typical,
sleepy Umbrian hill town.

occasion. The steps of the Duomo actually had to be washed down with wine and reconsecrated after one particularly horrific act of carnage, when the partisans of the Guelphs and the Ghibellines could not amicably settle their differences.

The *ganzi*, boisterous males who strut about the *piazze* in large groups during the lazy *passeggiata* hours, are not unlike the *consumatori della piazza* that Braccio Fortebraccio, who ruled

Perugia for eight years from 1416, so loathed. Mindful of the treachery of which the Perugians were capable, therefore wary of these 'idlers of the piazza', Braccio soon made plans for the employment of their spare time. He thoughtfully reintroduced an ancient 'game' called the Battle of Stones, which he quite rightly felt would divert any aggression that might be building up within his people during the (very rare) period of civic unity that he had created.

The Fontana Maggiore (top left) *beyond which is the battered but defiant lateral façade of the Duomo, Perugia. Scenes from the Creation relief on the façade of the Duomo, Orvieto* (bottom left).

On a chosen feast day, two teams had to fight for control of a piazza – any piazza – which was called the *campo di battaglia*. On these occasions one team, the *armati*, would be heavily padded against assault, their heads protected by helmets shaped like sparrow hawks. They would aim to stave off attacks from the other team, the *lanciatori*, who would throw rocks at them in an effort to kill or maim them. This charming sport took the Perugians' minds off their various vendettas for as long as eight years, though after the death of Braccio they again plunged back into discord and violence.

Nowadays the Perugians' aggressive spirit vents its fury and energy in the traffic jams that clog this overcrowded city. This is most obvious in the morning because everyone insists on driving to work, and at midday because, again, everyone insists on driving home to lunch, in the full knowledge that the *centro storico* is closed

In the half light of morning, the silhouette of Perugia cannot have changed much since Goethe's visit in 1786.

to motorized traffic. Screams of rage and abuse are exchanged by these antisocial drivers, all of them mindful of the fact that only one in three cars is likely to find a parking space.

The *centro storico* is very irregular, full of narrow, convoluted streets and passages, steep flights of shallow steps and lumpy hills, which make shopping and sightseeing arduous and tiring. The buildings have a ravaged look, like victorious dogs after a particularly savage fight. The houses behind the Palazzo dei Priori, a huge gaunt medieval public building on the west side of the Piazza IV Novembre, are all built like fortresses. Scarred, cracked façades with tiny windows rise up like cliffs along the ravine-like streets in what must be the most atmospheric city in Umbria. In the evenings the restless character of Perugia is left behind in the Corso Vannucci and the Piazza IV Novembre, among the *ganzi* and the girls strutting backwards and forwards, laughing and yelling to one another, while in the gloom and the shadows of the poorly lit Via dei Priori, and the streets leading off it, the ghosts of Perugia's past come alive. Footsteps of invisible figures can be heard in adjacent unseen alleys. In the Via Gabbia the wind rushes through the funnel between the top of the Palazzo dei Priori and the neighbouring *palazzi*, a silent but invigorating spirit in a street where a cage containing prisoners was once suspended. Here, poor unfortunate souls, generally criminals, languished on high in all weathers until they died.

Another street characteristic of Perugia is the via Ercolana, which leads to the Via Marzia (and the Etruscan Porta Marzia), where there is a twice-weekly market (Tuesdays and Saturdays). Sant'Ercolana, the patron saint of Perugia, was decapitated by Totila on the site of the octagonal church that commemorates her, which is squeezed in between the surrounding buildings. Further on is the Museo Archeologico Nazionale dell'Umbria, next to the church of San Domenico. While the museum contains collections of Etruscan artefacts from Perugia's past, the Galleria Nazionale dell'Umbria, at the top of the Palazzo dei Priori, contains the most important collection of Umbrian painting in Italy. Among the many other artistic masterpieces to be seen in Perugia is the Collegio del Cambio, underneath the Palazzo dei Priori. The walls of this fifteenth-century hall, used by members of the medieval money exchange, were frescoed by Perugino.

Perugia is a university town, with several thousand students enrolled in its various faculties. Apart from this, the ordinary state university, there is the Università degli Stranieri, the University for Foreigners, based in the Palazzo Gallenga in Piazza Fortebraccio, just outside one of the Etruscan city gates. This was set up in the late Twenties, and its existence draws a very cosmopolitan crowd of people to the city. Consequently there is a wide range of places to eat in Perugia, from the absurdly expensive to run of the mill dirt cheap. La Taverna, in the Via delle Streghe, is one of the former, with excellent, fairly traditional, Italian food, while in the latter category is Peppino, in the Via Danzetta. At Peppino's, the classic 'greasy spoon' cafe with a homely, busy atmosphere, I just ate chunks of Umbrian prosciutto and drank something rough and local from a flask. La Taverna, on the other hand, is the kind of place you would take your mistress to for a night out, and there I squirmed under the watchful stares of single female diners who presumably had been abandoned.

About twenty-five kilometres north-east of Perugia lies Gubbio, originally just as fierce and nearly as powerful as her neighbour. Out on a limb, in remote north-eastern Umbria, access is less easy than it is to other parts of the countryside. Apart from the physiognomy of the landscape, the roads are poorer than most. What is more, the nearest railway station is nineteen kilometres away, at Fossato di Vico (Rome–Ancona line), though a frequent bus

service runs between the two points.

This remoteness has meant that the forces of change have been less exacting on Gubbio's architectural heritage than elsewhere in the region. As a result, and in spite of its location, it is one of the most popular towns in Umbria, though the brasher effects of tourism seem to have kept their distance. Gubbio has some of Umbria's best restaurants, like the Taverna del Lupo in the Via G. Ansider, and the Fornace di Maestro Giorgio in the Via Maestro Giorgio. Both have a wide range of traditional food and both are in medieval settings. The former is in a thirteenth-century building and the latter on the site of a workshop that once belonged to Maestro Giorgio, the sixteenth-century ceramicist who discovered how to create a beautiful ruby-red lustre for his maiolica. In both, huge portions of such things as boar sausage or pigeon with olives and red wine fill you to bursting point. There is never any shortage of game in this area as the local forests are trawled relentlessly every year during the hunting season. White truffles, black truffles, risotto with truffles, lasagna with prosciutto and truffles, *carpaccio* with truffles – most of these and other variations can be had at the better restaurants. Gubbio is the home of the Umbrian white truffle. If you can't get enough of the fresh variety, you can always buy them in cans or jars, which can be found in abundance in the food shops lining the Via dei Consoli, on the way up to the Piazza Signoria.

Gubbio has some of the most forbidding military architecture in Italy. From afar the town is a solid, compacted mass of dusty, sunburnt houses straddling the lower slopes of Monte Ingino, way beneath the Basilica of Sant'Ubaldo. The entire town is dominated by the aggressive shape of the Palazzo dei Consoli, and the streets to it are steep and awkward. Apart from the TV aerials, and the traffic roaring up

A cantina, *Orvieto* (above). (Overleaf) *The early morning sun glints on the mosaics of the façade of the Duomo, Orvieto.*

and down the one-way system in the narrow winding lanes, there is nothing particularly twentieth-century about Gubbio. Development came to a halt in the Middle Ages as resources dried up and, street by street, it is exclusively and completely medieval. But whereas Perugia has managed, by an adroit bit of juggling, to maintain its ancient status as an important hill town and yet still become a slick, cosmopolitan modern city, Gubbio has slumped to the point where it is now nothing more than a benign backwater, its buildings the only reminder of an illustrious past.

From the Piazza Quaranta Martiri at the foot of the town, with its daily market, closed at one end by the old Logge Tiratori, streets ascend past ancient alleys and steep cobbled stairways to the Piazza della Signoria. The streets of Gubbio are interesting and varied, and the buildings lining them rise and fall with the contours of the hill, their builders having had no worries about uniformity of façade or consistency of height. Except for a few towers that were not razed either by enemies or by legislation, none of the houses are tall, and sometimes, from between them, you catch sudden views of the Umbrian countryside stretching far into the distance.

This strange, tantalizing glimpse of the Middle Ages is enlivened each year on 15 May when, dressed in medieval costume and waving medieval banners, the citizens of Gubbio race

up a gravel path to Sant'Ubaldo's basilica, which overlooks the town. This traditional festival is known as the *Corsa dei Ceri*. Its origins are ancient and unknown, but it is supposed to commemorate the death of Sant'Ubaldo, who is patron saint of the town. On the eve of the *festa*, the Gubbians drag out Ubaldo's unputrefied, if slightly mouldy, corpse for its annual airing, proceeding with it, in as dignified a manner as the situation will allow, down to the Duomo. Careering madly around its glass and gilt casket on its way to town, the saintly remains, dressed in bishop's vestments, are Gubbio's equivalent of a mascot.

What follows is a very strange mixture of pseudo-phallic rite of Spring and homage to Sant'Ubaldo. Three teams of ten men carry the *ceri*, three tall (ten-metre long) and immensely heavy wood and canvas 'candles', each one topped by a wax saint, to the Piazza della Signoria for the start of a race to the Sanctuary of Sant'Ubaldo, at the top of Monte Ingino. Apart from Ubaldo himself (a likeness only, not the corpse), there is San Giorgio and Sant'Antonio Abate, each one representing one of the town's guilds. Before the race begins, the corpse and the *ceri* are blessed by the Bishop of Gubbio. Then, each team rushes away as fast as their respective dead weights will allow, round the Piazza della Signoria, and up the hill to the sanctuary. It is irrelevant which one gets to the top of the hill first because Sant'Ubaldo, as patron saint, must always win. The team of San Giorgio is always second and Sant'Antonio Abate third.

The whole town throws itself vigorously into this festival. It is an unforgettable experience, all the more so because of its high drama (enhanced by carafes of red wine) and the fact that Sant'Ubaldo is present, as it were, in the flesh. The crowds lining the streets along the route to Monte Ingino draw back as the race passes by, then surge forward as necks are craned to get a better view. There is a tension in

Beyond Assisi, the great central Umbrian valley and, in the distance, the hill town of Spello.

the air as everyone, transfixed by the waxen figures teetering wildly on their pole tops, is suddenly silent. Then the moment of suspense passes – the saints never fall – and a relaxed babble overtakes the onlookers as the teams rush on.

Feste are the occasions when Gubbio's young, who have left town to get work elsewhere, migrate back to their family's crumbling homes, bringing their washing with them. Before their arrival mothers are seen shaking dust out of carpets, and airing blankets and bedding out of gothic windows, while down below, bars and cafes, more ancient than anyone can remember, serve chunks of *porchetta* (roast pork) between two slabs of crusty bread, just as they always have.

Out on a limb, locked into its rural landscape, Gubbio is far away from the other important little hill towns – Assisi, Spello, Trevi and Montefalco – that crowd the central valley between Perugia and Spoleto. Assisi is perhaps the best known of them. Here, stretched along the side of Monte Subasio, is the small town in which St Francis was born. Linked to the outside world by a railway line about five kilometres away, Assisi today is much frequented by pilgrims and sightseers. Its tiny cobbled streets are lined by a series of austere façades, with external flights of steps and wrought-iron work. In many ways it is not unlike the other Umbrian hill towns of its period – ancient, walled and pinkish-brown in colour – except that it is quieter (at night) and far less steep. Here the cult of St Francis survives not in the detached way that a community preserves a relic under the altar but as a living memory. His cult, as patron saint of Assisi (and, since 1939, of Italy as well) nearly eclipses the town's secular past. It was once a belligerent place, in the Perugian tradition, subject to the usual inter-family disputes, vendettas, plague and famine.

During the day it is awash with visitors, but after dark, when the streets have resumed their ancient stillness and shadowy light, the spirit of St Francis is always close at hand. Distant footsteps or the yowling of a cat are the only things that break the nocturnal silence.

Franciscan history and the Franciscan legend are the only reasons the town survives at all. St Francis cracked the strict hierarchy of the Church, driving a wedge through an organization that was on the verge of moral bankruptcy. His simple religion of love had such mass appeal that it was rapidly institutionalized by the Church in Rome, and the town became a shrine to his memory. His remains are in the Basilica of San Francesco, along with some of the greatest paintings the early Italian Renaissance ever produced. Indeed here are some of the very first paintings to emerge from the gloom of the Middle Ages – works by Cimabue, Giotto, Pietro Lorenzetti and Simone Martini.

On almost every day of the week, coaches line up in the piazza below the basilica to unload their charges, who scuttle off like chickens to gorge themselves on the far-distant views of the great Umbrian plain. There are groups of nuns from all over the world, and southern Italian women who come not to see, or even to attempt to understand, the great frescoes in the basilica.

*A*ssorted remains of Assisi's past.

They come to make contact with the patron saint of Italy and to pray in front of his tomb. With tears in their eyes, as silently they finger their rosaries, they have an untainted childlike simplicity of which the saint himself would have approved.

Outside, in the Via San Francesco, are the Saint Francis souvenir shops: rosaries made of olive wood, Saint Francis ceramics, great pasta dishes, from the bottom of which the saint can be seen wagging his finger at you, and bits of plastic covered with scenes from the Giotto frescos line the pavement. In glass cases nailed to the outside walls of the shops are vulgar statuettes of nuns lifting their habits. None of this would have pleased St Clare, the female counterpart, and contemporary, of St Francis.

St Clare founded the Poor Clares, whose role originally was to beg for the Franciscan friars. The church of San Damiano, a little way out of town, where Saint Francis received his calling to 'rebuild God's Church', was once home to the Poor Clares. The nuns moved to the Basilica of Santa Chiara in the thirteenth century, taking their founder's body with them. There it can be seen to this day, now blackened by age.

Assisi's calendar is more crowded with *feste* than any other town in Italy. One is the Calendimaggio, a medieval celebration, which takes place on the last day of April, and commemorates St Francis's past with songs, dances, competitions between Upper and Lower Assisi and torchlight processions. There is another on 22 June, the Feast of the Holy Vow, which celebrates Saint Clare's saving of the city from the Saracens, and a variety of others range from medieval tournaments (the Palio della Balestra on 11 August) to music festivals.

For such a small town, Assisi is also very well endowed with museums. Apart from the churches, which are practically art galleries in themselves, there is the Museo-Tesoro della Basilica, behind the Basilica di San Francesco, which has a large collection of Renaissance paintings and religious paraphernalia, the Pinacoteca Civica, in the Palazzo Comunale, with a collection of Umbrian Renaissance art, and the Museo Civico, in the Piazza del Comune, which displays bits of Assisi's Roman forum and some statuary from the Etruscan period.

Many of the smaller Umbrian hill towns, like Spello, on another flank of Monte Subiaso, about fifteen kilometres from Assisi, seem to be an integral part of the countryside around them. Although Spello is still contained within its old walls, it is a typical example of a town inhabited by people who work on the land. Rather than live in farmhouses out among the crops, the people of Spello are urban dwellers out of habit rather than because they need the security that their ancestors found there. Their relationship with the land is a specialist one; they indulge in a system of part-time farming that allows them to leave the town at dawn and to work in the fields until lunch-time, returning only late in the afternoon to finish off their work. At one time they would have kept their animals in the stables beneath their houses, taking them to the fields at day-break and returning with them in the evening. Nowadays, since the only hazards for livestock in the Italian countryside are likely to derive from pollution, the animals stay out all the time.

As I picked my way through the jumble of Spello's monumental past, skirting ancient crumbling houses and bits of classical architecture holding up Renaissance doorways, the loudest sounds emanating from the heart of its maze of medieval alleys came from chickens and geese penned behind the wire netting stretched across ancient portals and derelict courtyards. Sudden wider spaces are occupied by goats. The weekly market is full of produce cultivated in allotments abutting the town walls, or in gardens squeezed into patches between the buildings, wherever the sun shines. There are also flowers and shrubs, but generally horti-

There is a tremendous amount of detail on the façade of the Duomo – marble reliefs describe episodes from the Old and New Testaments, and there are scenes from the Life of the Virgin, Christ and the Saints in mosaic.

culture in these little towns is a subsistence activity, handed down through generations of country people, who in the past were often incarcerated for months under siege behind their city walls.

A couple of hours in Spello would be enough to take in Pinturicchio's fresco cycle in Santa Maria Maggiore's Baglioni chapel and still leave time for a meal at either Il Molino, in the Piazza Matteotti, or the Rosticceria La Torre, in the Piazza JF Kennedy at the foot of the town. The Roman Porta Consolare overlooks the latter, a busy, lively cafe serving ordinary, delicious things. I gorged myself on *peperoni arrosti, carciofi fritti* and *coniglio arrosto* (roast peppers, artichoke fritters and roast rabbit).

With a population of only 7000, Spello is a quiet, gentle town, though its proximity to the highway means that it does not have the sense of abandonment and isolated silence that one feels at Montefalco, just a few kilometres down the road to the south. Called the 'balcony' of Umbria, Montefalco is 473 metres up, and from its tower, way above the old brown roof tops and the chestnuts, a wide panorama extends the entire length of the valley.

Montefalco once earned itself the title of 'a little strip of heaven fallen to earth' because in the Middle Ages, even though it was dominated by one power after another, fought over, ravaged, sacked and finally grabbed by the Church after ferocious fighting, the citizens managed to keep their wits about them and preserve a degree of calm. During this period it produced eight saints, all most probably inspired in their religious mysticism by the strange, isolated silence of their town, up among the clouds. The Middle Ages also spawned a phenomenal quantity of religious painting in Montefalco, most of it concentrated in the churches of Sant'Agostino and San Francesco.

The town today is not much different from the day Benozzo Gozzoli included it in the St Francis frescoes cycle which he painted in the church of San Francesco in the middle of the fifteenth century. It shows St Francis blessing a group of citizens from Montefalco, who kneel in front of him on a hillside outside the city walls. Behind rise the churches and towers of the city, sharply outlined against the hills on the far side of the valley. Below them the ground falls away steeply to the plain, while in the distance is Assisi. Gozzoli was right: on a clear day you can see Assisi to the north-east, as well as Spello and Trevi on the opposite side of the valley.

St Francis would still find peace and quiet in Montefalco, for now it is practically deserted. Only old men sit gossiping in a sunny patch and widows in black shop in Via Umberto, the single street running down to Porta Sant'Agostino. Here there is also a bar where you can taste the local *sagrantino*, a strong, sweet sherry-like red wine only made in and around Montefalco.

South of Spello and Montefalco are Trevi and Spoleto, the latter the home of the Festival of the Two Worlds, an annual (June to July) festival of the arts, which was set up by Giancarlo Menotti in 1957. In western Umbria, at the bottom of the Tiber valley is the town of Todi, about thirty kilometres to the west of the last great outpost of the region, Orvieto. When Edward Hutton went to Todi before the last war, he found 'one of the great surprises of Umbria'. It still is in a way, though it is no longer the 'silent and neglected' city of his day. Like Spoleto, it is the annual setting for a series of concerts and exhibitions, which are held here for about ten days in September. Hordes of people come to Todi for the festival, hovering in the Piazza del Popolo or sitting outside the Gran Caffè del Duomo and drinking green cocktails from coloured glasses, wine and *caffè*. Hutton's 'great and beautiful Piazza', with the romanesque Duomo at the top of a long flight of steps at one end and a superb array of miniature medieval buildings at the other, is a perfect auditorium, providing concerts and ballet performances with a magnificent natural stage set, which is enhanced by selective spotlighting on the crenellations, mullioned windows and towers of the surrounding buildings.

All this is much appreciated by the audience who, when I was there, were media types from Rome – faux blondes with a great deal of gold jewellery, Etruscan style, and fashion-plate men with shoulder-padded leather jackets. Each evening they stood about in packs, smoking and cruising one another while listening to the music used for testing the sound equipment. During these moments the venerable old piazza reverberated with the hoarse sound of Eros Ramazotti and the more youthful tones of Jovanotti, two of Italy's current heart-throb pop stars with their drop dead looks.

Todi sits on one of the oldest occupied sites in Umbria. A shaky legend insists that the spot was chosen when an eagle, who had swooped down and stolen a cloth from an ancient Umbrian family, dropped it further away, at the top of the hill. Todi's insignia is still that of an eagle with its wings outstretched and a cloth between its claws. Contrarily, another legend is equally insistent that the town marks the site where Hercules killed Caco.

At about 410 metres, the balustrade of the Piazza Garibaldi, looking eastwards out over the lemon trees in the gardens below, offers the best views over the hazy countryside. I just sat out on the terrace of the Ristorante Umbria (it has the same view), the entrance to which is buried in the cavernous undercroft of the Palazzo del Capitano. Visitors to the town are never really aware of the town's height until their calf muscles are taxed in the climb up the Via Matteotti, from the Porta Romana to the Piazza del Popolo. Although, after Cortona, Todi was chicken feed.

Cars should be left outside the gates of the town and, if the walk up from the Porta Romana is too steep, you can always park near Santa Maria della Consolazione, a church said to be a simplified version of Bramante's design for St

Peter's in Rome. From here, take one of the little orange buses up the Via Cerquette to the Piazza della Repubblica, below the church of San Fortunato. Here, inside the three concentric rings of walls surrounding Todi, are the little medieval streets of pinkish-brown buildings and irregular *piazze* which characterize the three miniature districts of the town. One, the Valle Inferiore, is always being threatened by landslides, and it is interesting to note that this is the one district of the town that is not supported by the original Roman wall; in other parts of the town the wall, which Vitruvius pointed out as being a notable example of good building, is still standing.

Todi's one great claim to fame is that it was the home of perhaps the greatest Franciscan poet, Fra Jacopone Benedetti, who composed verses in the vernacular in the thirteenth century. These were easily understood by the townspeople and the peasants, and their humanizing influence contained much of the Franciscan message. Naturally he became very popular. Fra Jacopone's dramatic conversion from avaricious man about Todi to tertiary of the Franciscan Order, intent on a life of mortification and penance, came about when he found that his wife, who fell off a platform and died during a hectic wedding feast, had been wearing a hair shirt beneath her finery. Joining the more spiritual branch of the Franciscans, he was thrown into a dungeon for five years by Pope

Piazza del Popolo from the Duomo; Todi is still one of the 'great surprises of Umbria'.

Boniface VIII for opposing the corruption of the papacy. He also denounced the Pope as the 'new Lucifer', which didn't help his cause. The courageous Fra Jacopone is remembered today by a pie called the *Pasticcio di Jacopone* which is made, appropriately enough, in the Ristorante Jacopone in the Piazza Jacopone. Generally cone shaped, the pastry is filled with meat, vegetables, ricotta, eggs, cheese and a sprinkling of unspecified, and secret, spices.

Going west from Todi, the SS 448 runs in the direction of Orvieto, taking you along the banks, and for a while the gorge, of the Tiber, towards the AI autostrada which goes to Rome. To the north of Todi the E45 leads to Perugia, which is 42 kilometres away. As with most small towns in Umbria, Todi has no station close at hand, though four kilometres away is a small single track line which will connect you, extremely slowly, with Terni in the south-east, and with Perugia.

Even though these Umbrian hill towns lost their independence more than four hundred years ago, and have been submerged in a united Italy for more than a century now, their citizens maintain a degree of pride and a sense of their own individuality that emerges when the surface of their communities is gently scratched. Old habits die hard in Umbria, so do old rivalries, in the isolation of the hills, away from the mainstream of Italian life. Now that Perugia is the regional capital, guarding the centralized bureaucracy within its battlemented and warlike Palazzo Comunale, the Perugians can afford to indulge in a little of the dictatorial behaviour of their ancestors. This enflames ancient enmities, especially when the Perugians decide what happens in Assisi or allocate funds inappropriately in Todi. The people of Gubbio feel that they are still the victims of their old enemies in Perugia who, in their opinion, have monopolized the tourist trade, forgetting to maintain, or to enlarge, the routes to their own town, one of the last outposts of the region.

*T*odi sits on one of the oldest occupied sites in Umbria.

THE MARCHES

URBINO · SAN LEO · GRADARA · LORETO
MACERATA

Giovanni Santi, Raphael's father, and a painter himself, filled the backgrounds of his works with landscapes of stylized hills, tightly cropped trees in silhouette and winding country roads. Here and there, scattered about, he painted in the occasional chapel or cluster of reddish brick farm buildings. Considering that Santi was painting in the second half of the fifteenth century, it is remarkable that the landscape of The Marches region today has hardly changed. Even with a bit of artistic licence, and Santi was well versed in the tradition of fancifully lyrical scenes, it is not difficult to imagine the delight with which he beheld these surroundings.

Mostly mountainous, with some of the highest peaks of the Apennine range along Monti Sibillini in the west, the steeper uplands of The Marches turn into gentler hills towards the Adriatic. The landscape of this region, hemmed in between Emilia Romagna, Umbria and the Abruzzo, is lyrical and splendid and, while the paintings of Santi tend to emphasize the lyricism and only toy with the splendour, it is also remarkably panoramic.

From towns like San Leo and Cingoli, high on their rocky crags, San Leo 600 metres high, Cingoli 631 metres, you can see for miles over woodland and ploughed fields edged with neat, dark cypresses. The winding roads of The Marches of Santi's imagination (which can be seen in his paintings in the Galleria Nazionale delle Marche, in Urbino) lead the eye from the foreground of his pictures, with their saints and Madonnas, to vistas of isolated castles and fabled cities. While there is nothing fabled about Urbino or Macerata, two of the larger cities of the Marche, they are, like Santi's backgrounds, enveloped by a dreamy bluish mist on most summer days, so that from afar you can see only the vaguest outlines of spires and domes.

The Marches are the one great undiscovered secret of central Italy. Except for the more popular hill towns like Urbino, and of course the resorts along the coast, the region is largely overlooked by outsiders. It is full of hill cities and silent hill villages – as in Umbria, mostly walled – remote fortresses, crumbling country sanctuaries full of fading, dewy-eyed Madon-

The Palazzo Ducale (above) rises clifflike above the approach to Urbino. To the right is a Renaissance portal, Urbino.

nas, and huge squat sixteenth-century farm-steads standing in isolated wooded valleys. Its major cities have examples of great art, and it has the kind of cooking that left me gasping for air as I tried to force down the very last mouthful of some gigantic helping of a delicious *Marchigiano* dish.

Time and energy are the prerequisites for a tour around The Marches. The only major route through the region is along the coast, following the autostrada, the A14, which runs from Bologna to Bari in Apulia. All the other roads are a mere fraction of its size and efficiency, making travelling very slow. At intervals along the A14, wherever there is a major gap in the mountains and an accommodating valley to the west, secondary routes make an appearance, secondary in classification because of the threat from *caduta massi* – falling rocks from the hillsides above – and because of the precipitous drops on one side, which seem hellbent on enticing drivers over the edge.

Urbino lies on one such route, the SS 423, which leaves the coast at Pesaro; heaving and rolling past a variety of villages, it is eventually stopped dead in its tracks by Urbino itself, high on its mountain, inert but watchful, like a guard at a border crossing. A spectacular cliff-like edifice of pink-brown cut stone and brick, with great twin turrets and conical roofs and regular, mostly unadorned, windows faces the road on the edge of the town, above the old market place. This is the Palazzo Ducale, built by Federico da Montefeltro, Duke of Urbino, in the fifteenth century. It dominates the town entirely, reducing, to the point of insignificance, virtually every other building there, including the Duomo in the Piazza Ducale, next to one of the palace entrances. Even if you come from Tuscany, along the winding SS 73 from Bocca Trabaria – where Tuscany, Umbria and The Marches meet – and pass through the small town of Urbania, straight to Urbino's main entrance at the Porta di Valbona, you see the

The Palazzo Ducale, Urbino.

massive bulk of the palace before anything else.

To Baldassare Castiglione, who was in Urbino in the sixteenth century, the Palazzo Ducale was a city within a city. Nowadays it contains the Galleria Nazionale delle Marche and the Istituto di Belle Arti. You enter the rambling building via the Cortile d'Onore and a vast staircase, up which grandees would ride their horses to the great state chambers above. During the reign of Federico, Urbino rose to become one of the most distinguished centres of Renaissance culture and, under his son Guidobaldo, its palace became the epicentre of the Montefeltro dukedom's Golden Age. In the same league as Cosimo de' Medici and Pope Pius II Piccolomini, this second Duke of Urbino was both unconquerable lord and learned prince. He built up his little state, which extended as far as San Leo in the north, making it the seat for the best art and scholarship of the time and not just the base of a powerful fiefdom.

Guidobaldo and his wife, Elisabetta Gonzaga, attracted almost every famous architect, sculptor, painter, man of letters and intellectual of the *quattrocento* and the early *cinquecento* to Urbino. The most significant among them were Luciano Laurana, Francesco di Giorgio Martini, Piero della Francesca, Giusto di Gand and Domenico Rosselli. The artistic treasures housed in the Palazzo Ducale were second to none, and it is only a very small proportion of the original painting collection that survives here today as the nucleus of the Galleria Nazionale. Apart from works by Piero della Francesca, including the well-known *Flagellation*, there is also the strange painting by an unknown hand (possibly della Francesca, or alternatively Laurana) called *The Ideal City*. Other significant works by Paolo Uccello, Signorelli, Raphael, Luca della Robbia and Giovanni Santi, among others, are now kept here as well.

Castiglione was so impressed by what he found at Urbino that he used the city as the basis for his book *Il libro del cortegiano* (The book of the courtier); first published in 1528, this is perhaps the most widely known but least read book to have emerged from Renaissance Italy. In it Castiglione describes Urbino as the centre of the Italian peninsula 'on the Adriatic side …'. He centres the work round a fictional, but ideal, court and in many ways he provides an idealized portrait of Federico's court at Urbino, and models its descriptions on noble social gatherings here of Renaissance court society.

For all the grandeur and magnificence of its past, Urbino today seemed to me to be a provincial place, modest even and slightly sad. In spite of its university, whose population fills the squares and streets during the day, you do get the feeling that here is a city that relies too hard on its illustrious past to give it vigour and energy. To me Urbino is a stagnant city, which lost its way in the seventeenth century when it reverted to papal ownership, becoming part of the Papal States.

While life in the Piazza della Repubblica between 5.00 p.m. and 8.00 p.m. is the usual effervescence of voices, hooting and laughter provided by the time-wasters during their *passeggiata* break, Urbino has the look of a person from whose face the blood has been drained. Very neat and tidy, very well restored, in parts perhaps too well restored, its mixed *quattrocento-cinquecento* character primped and dusted to an unnatural degree, Urbino has been sealed in a timewarp of the age of Duke Federico and his immediate heirs, and today there is very little to change this.

If you sit drinking coffee outside the Caffè Centrale, in the Piazza della Repubblica, enveloped in the exhaust fumes of passing taxis, you may notice that the bustle of the town is only superficial. While there are shops and bars, concentrated mostly in the Via Mazzini, which connects the Porta di Valbona with the Piazza

Piazza Dante, San Leo.

della Repubblica, and there is the odd restaurant, a cinema or two and a theatre, life after dark in Urbino barely exists. The warren-like back streets, like the Via Posta Vecchia, the Via Volta della Morta and the Via della Morta are silent, shuttered and sad. In the latter a notice edged in black and gummed to the wall informs the neighbourhood that '*Salvatore Marra è tornato alla Case del Padre*' (that is, Salvatore Marra has returned to the House of God). I too nearly ended up at the gates of God's house after a scooter came hurtling out of a dark alley and threw its driver at me as it slipped on the frosty cobbles. Motorcycles and scooters are the bane of urban life in all Italian towns, and they are as noisy, air-polluting and antisocial, as they are popular.

There is, however, a lot for visitors to see and do in Urbino. Apart from visiting the various churches and the Palazzo Ducale, there is the Museo del Duomo and the Casa di Raffaello, the birthplace of Raphael in the Via Raffaello, containing a series of tableaux celebrating the painter's life. There are also some works by his father, pieces of period furniture and artefacts.

If you don't want an ice cream or a combination of ice creams from Arcobaleno in the Via Bramante, or want to gaze at the enormous dead pig, sliced clean in two with a meat cleaver, hanging upside down at the butcher's in the Via Raffaello, you can always go to the little shop at 44 Via Vittorio Veneto and buy a special chrome truffle cutter – a *tagliatartufi*. Or, after a walk among the box hedges in the neat public garden at the top of the town, where all Urbino's notables have been sculpted in bronze and placed on top of pedestals, hermlike in the ancient Roman fashion, you can lunch at Il Cortegiano or the Bramante.

San Leo lies about fifty-five kilometres north-west of Urbino, high on an enormous rocky spar. It was a fortress town belonging to Federico da Montefeltro, and as one of his military outposts, it represented the warlike aspect of his successful rule. San Leo's impregnability and dramatic situation, poised on the pinnacle of a sheer drop, nearly six hundred metres above the surrounding countryside, fired the imaginations of both Bembo and Machiavelli. Today the fortress itself is, infuriatingly, *chiuso per restauro* (closed for restoration) and no amount of pleading with the Pro Loco, based in the Palazzo Medici in the Piazza Dante, will give access to the interior, where Giuseppe Balsamo spent his last years.

This man, the self-styled Count of Cagliostro, earned his incarceration in this stout fortress prison at the end of the eighteenth century for some very dubious and fraudulent behaviour. Not only did he con people into believing that he had discovered a way of transforming base metals into gold but he also sold love potions, mixtures for making ugly women beautiful, and elixirs of youth which, he said, had kept him alive for thousands of years. His incarceration put an end to his knack, and he died here in 1795, locked in a cell.

The Pieve and the Duomo of San Leo date from the ninth and eleventh centuries respectively. Their interiors have that chilly mustiness which, though pleasant – even welcoming – in the summer, is tomblike in the winter. Late in the afternoons, when the *Marchigiani* gloom begins to deepen the shadows in the crypts, you can just about make out carved heads and beasts on the capitals of ancient decorated columns. In the sombre, cavernous depths of the Duomo you can examine bits of San Leo, who has obviously always been greatly revered here because the steps to his sarcophagus have been worn down to a treacherously shiny ramp by hundreds of tramping pilgrims' feet. San Leo is supposed to have taken refuge on this spot from persecution by Emperor Diocletian (his friend Marino doing the same just to the east, on another rocky crag now the Republic of San Marino), and since the fourth century this rock

has been central to his cult.

Other buildings of interest in this little town, on its lonely crag below Monte Carpegna, are the twelfth-century Torre, now the campanile for the Duomo, and the *palazzi* Nardini, Medici and Della Rovere. The Palazzo Nardini was the scene of the donation to St Francis of the sanctuary of La Verna by Count Orlando da Chiusi in 1213. The count, deeply impressed by St Francis's preaching and sincerity, gave the saint, who was passing by, and his friars 'Mount La Verna with all the land whether wooded, rocky or grassy without any exception, from the brow of the mountain to its foot …'. The other two *palazzi* represent varying fortunes in the history of the town.

San Leo is a rather dignified place, whose freshly laundered quality has been devised to give tourists maximum value for their money. Whereas in southern Italy you'll find beaten, bashed monuments, the wear and tear of the ages engrained into their fabric, here in San Leo there is nothing that is not looked after. Consequently, in a town with only about 2600 inhabitants, summertime sees the place awash with strangers, for whom the quaint charm of this *città d'arte* invariably proves irresistible. Its monuments are all scattered about within close proximity of the central Piazza Dante, with its Albergo/Ristorante Castello, and the Via Michele Rosa, with its Bar Cagliostro.

Each year a 'weekend' *gastronomico* is organized in the province of Urbino and Pesaro, which includes San Leo. At a variety of locations around the countryside a chosen restaurant agrees to produce a specific menu of local dishes on an agreed date. At San Leo this normally happens in June, and the Ristorante La Rocca, in the Strada del Forte, will produce, for example, for a first course, *tortelloni di San Leo alla Rocca* or *strozzapreti alla villana* (which literally means something which chokes priests and is cooked in a rustic style). Other menus around the countryside are rather more elabor-

*O*fficialdom, Macerata-style (above). *A cluster of*
Medieval houses (overleaf) *beneath the Palazzo Ducale.*

ate, and you would have to ask at a major tourist office (in Urbino or Pesaro) for details, menus and specific dates.

San Leo is not connected with any railway route, though precipitous country lanes link it to the SS 258, which leads to the Republic of San Marino not far away. There is a bus service to Rimini, and from here you can take the A14 motorway, which runs along the Adriatic coast to two other little hill towns, Gradara, a walled town north of Pesaro, and Novilara, just a little way to the south.

Gradara was the scene of a tragic drama that ran its course seven hundred years ago. In the thirteenth century, the Malatesta lords of Rimini and the Polenta lords of Ravenna decided to form an alliance, and to this end arranged the marriage of Gianciotto Malatesta to Francesca Polenta. The former was ugly and old, so the story goes, and the latter a young child. Aware of the fact that Francesca would most probably refuse her suitor, who was also deformed, the Malatesta sent Paolo, Gianciotto's younger and very much more handsome brother to the wedding to stand proxy. Francesca fell in love with Paolo 'Il Bello' who, by all accounts, was a heart-throb who was easily flattered; a romance developed that was taken to its logical conclusion in a feudal bed-chamber somewhere deep in the castle of Gradara. Unfortunately, these events were observed by a servant, who told Gianciotto what was taking place; enraged, Gianciotto rushed home and murdered both Francesca and Paolo.

Dante puts the lovers in the second circle of Hell, the part of his Inferno reserved for carnal sinners, thus giving the story the permanence of a legend; in fact without Dante this tragedy would never have been remembered. Today you can visit the castle and look out through the battlements on which Francesca probably wandered as she waited for her lover's visits.

Continuing further south along the A14, past Ancona, is Loreto, an outpost for the cult of the Virgin, and the most popular pilgrimage site in Italy after Rome. The principal object of attention for the pilgrim is the Santa Casa, the Virgin's house, which 'flew' to this spot in the thirteenth century. The devout celebrate this incredible event annually with an immense procession, which ends with the lighting of bonfires on the hilltops around the town. The sacred 'relic' of the Virgin still survives, encased in marble by Bramante, and now housed under the dome of the huge Santuario della Santa Casa, designed by Giovanni Boccalini and Giovan Battista Ghioldi. This basilica occupies one side of Loreto's central Piazza della Madonna, which is an eloquent showcase of the work of some of Italy's finest artists and architects. Apart from its façade, the basilica is a mixture of the work of Bramante, Antonio da Sangallo il Giovane and Andrea Sansovino. Internally, there are decorations by Melozzo da Forli in the Sacristy of San Marco and by Signorelli in the Sacristy of San Giovanni.

The fountain in front of the great church, with its bronze tritons riding the backs of leaping dolphins, was designed by Carlo Maderno and Giovanni Fontana. As if all of this weren't enough, to the left of the church is the Palazzo Apostolico, with its two-tiered loggia, which was started by Bramante and worked on by Antonio da Sangallo: the strange campanile, northern European in style, was designed in the eighteenth century by Vanvitelli.

Montaigne came here in 1581 and remarked on the quantity of goods on sale, from wax images to beads and *salvators* (medals or images of the Lamb of God). Nothing much has changed today. Satisfied pilgrims return triumphantly from the Corso Boccalini to their homes all over Italy – practically nobody ever comes to Loreto but Italians – armed with rosaries, Virgins garlanded with plastic flowers and crucifixes.

To the south-west and further inland is Macerata, a large walled town with one of the twelve oldest universities in Italy. It has all the hub and din of a city, with students, shoppers, the clatter of heels on cobbles and general traffic confusion contributing to, and enlivening, the otherwise low key atmosphere of the place. In fact, scattered over its low mound between the Potenza and the Chienti rivers, roughly twenty kilometres from the sea, Macerata has only about 45,000 inhabitants, though this number swells during term time. The town's most significant claim to fame is the fact that it was the scene of Bonnie Prince Charlie's marriage to Princess Louise of Stolberg in 1772. The chapel register notes that he signed himself Charles III of Great Britain, France and Ireland.

In one of Macerata's more gulley-like streets is the Trattoria da Natale Ezio: follow the signs from the Rampa Zara, an opening in the northern length of the city wall, off the Viale Giacomo Leopardi. Here, as in any one of the city's many *trattorie* or restaurants, you will find *cucina tipica Marchigiana*. This, I found, includes *brodetto*, The Marches version of fish soup, made with things like squid, eel, red mullet, sea bass and sole, and sometimes Adriatic specialities such as *cannocchie*, a flat-tailed crustacean. Cooked with garlic, tomato, onion, parsley and vinegar, it also has a pinch of saffron for colouring. There might also be *caciotto*, a local cheese made from cow's and sheep's milk, or *salame Fabriano* made from a mixture of pork meat and *vitellone*, young beef. Practically every neighbourhood in Italy has its own *cucina tipica*, but universal in this particular region is a gluttonous desire to stuff everything with everything else – for example *coniglio in porchetta* (stuffed roast rabbit) or pigeons stuffed with black olives and black olives stuffed with chicken.

A breakfast of *caffè macchiato* (espresso coffee with a drop of milk) and a *cornetto* (a pastry stuffed with either custard or marmalade) – both universal throughout the country – can be had at the Bar Centrale, in the Piazza della Libertà, at the very top of the town, where the *vie* Matteotti, Gramsci and della Repubblica branch off in their separate directions. Apart from the permanent exhibition of *presepi* (cribs, Neapolitan-style, in the museum in the Via Maffeo Pantaleoni) and the Pinacoteca Comunale in Piazza Vittorio Veneto, there isn't a great deal to detain a visitor in Macerata. After a last look at Crivelli's *Madonna* in San Giovanni, you will probably choose to move on into the province of Macerata, which is full of more peaceful, smaller hill towns.

Though most are medieval, if not in their entirety then almost certainly at their centres, all have their own peculiarities. There is Treia to the north-west and Cingoli beyond, both the colour of baked clay. Cingoli is blessed with the title *Balcone delle Marche* since, over 600 metres high, it dominates the wooded hills and ploughed fields of light brown clay of the central Marche for many miles around. These uplands fall away gently towards the sea beyond Loreto.

To the south-east lie Sant'Elpidio a Mare and Fermo, the latter only six kilometres from the sea. Fermo has tremendous views to the Adriatic on one side and to the impressive Gran Sasso range of the Apennines in the Abruzzo on the other.

The Rocca menacing the countryside above the town of San Leo.

VENETO

ASOLO · CONEGLIANO · POSSAGNO
FELTRE · BELLUNO · ARQUA PETRARCA

The area known as Venetia is divided into three regions. Once called the Three Venetos, it is made up of the old Venezia Euganea, now called the Veneto, and the two semi-autonomous regions of Trentino-Alto Adige and Friuli Venezia-Giulia, and it stretches from the River Po to the Dolomites and from Lake Garda to Yugoslavia.

The Veneto is perhaps the most interesting of these three regions. Quantities of literary and artistic ghosts haunt some of its hill towns. There is always some annual event celebrating an artistic achievement, and not a year goes by without marking somebody's centenary. It doesn't make the slightest difference if the object of civic adulation wasn't born in the town; just living there for a few years is enough, provided your achievements extended further than the town's outer limits.

Asolo, a small town about forty kilometres north-west of Venice, is perhaps the best known of the hill towns of the Veneto, with a list of literary affiliations ranging from Pietro Bembo, the fifteenth-century cardinal and humanist, to Robert Browning (it has a Via Browning). It

doesn't have a native figure to adore, but has borrowed Freya Stark, who still lives there, and made her an honorary citizen. The towns of Possagno, Conegliano, Arqua Petrarca and Pieve di Cadore also nostalgically uphold their links with the past. Possagno, a few kilometres north of Asolo, was the home of the eighteenth-century sculptor Antonio Canova, and the painter Cima, a contemporary of Titian, lived at Conegliano. Titian himself, the greatest of the Venetian painters, was born at Pieve di Cadore, much further north, beyond Belluno, in the Cadore mountains. Arqua Petrarca, south-west of Padua, in the Euganean Hills, was the town to which Petrarch escaped from the rigours of metropolitan Padua in 1374. His house, and his stuffed cat, can still be visited.

There is no doubt that many of the outsiders who came to live in the Veneto were attracted to the area by its landscape. The southern portion of the region, except for a few small pockets of hilly areas, is completely flat. This is the Pianura Padana (which Shelley calls 'the green sea … the waveless plain …'), the basin of Italy's largest river, the Po. It stretches across

Asolo (above) *and the gardens of the Villa Contarini* (right).

the southern Veneto to the Adriatic, whose waters once lapped the base of the volcanic Euganean Hills. Going north, the region erupts first into the gentle sub-Alpine hills around Asolo and Possagno, and finally bursts skywards through the jagged needle-pointed Dolomites, in the midst of which is Pieve di Cadore. The hills of Asolo, Possagno and Conegliano are low humps fringed with stone crenellations and cypresses, while Pieve di Cadore lies on the side of a dramatic slope, which falls away to the Piave River and the Lago di Pieve di Cadore way below.

I don't suppose that Asolo is any bigger now than it was in Pietro Bembo's day. Contained by the slopes of the Colli Asolani – a handful of lumpen mounds which are a foretaste, though only on a tiny scale, of the Alpine foothills around Monte Grappa – the town is incapable of expanding in any rational way. The Via Browning, Asolo's main street, winds up through the Porta Loreggia, past a former home of Freya Stark, the Villa Freya, and past Robert Browning's house, opposite the Fontanella Zen; it then enters the Piazza Giuseppe Garibaldi, whose fifteenth-century fountain, built from Roman fragments, is surmounted by the lion of San Marco, the symbol of Venice. Lining the route up to the piazza are a variety of arches, colonnades, gothic windows Venetian-style and frescoed façades. To one side is the church of Santa Maria di Breda (which contains a painting by Lorenzo Lotto of the Assumption, and others by painters of the Venetian school) while, higher up, the piazza stretches as far as the formal gardens of the Villa Scotti Pasini, a typical Palladian-style villa. Tottering above the church and looming over the piazza, are the remains of the castle of Asolo, once the property of Catherine Cornaro, Queen of Cypress, Jerusalem and Armenia.

This unfortunate woman, a member of one of Venice's great patrician families, was forced to marry Giacomo II, King of Cypress,

Jerusalem and Armenia, in the middle of the fifteenth century, and was then shunted off to Cypress. She gave birth to a son, who died, followed closely by its father; the Venetians then brought her back to Venice 'for political reasons', giving her Asolo as compensation. She arrived on 11 October 1489 with a guard of a hundred Venetian soldiers and a black dwarf to keep her company.

Pietro Bembo was the queen's cousin and, for a while, her secretary. His dialogues, *Gli Asolani*, are supposed to document the opinions of the Queen's courtiers. They reflect life at her court which was famed for its intellectual activity and the *joie de vivre* of its nobles, artists and other writers. Bembo even coined a new verb, *asolare*, which basically means to have a good time and amuse oneself.

Queen Catherine was the presiding figure on Bembo's stage, and in *Gli Asolani* he carefully describes the garden of the castle, in which the dialogues took place: the steps descending from the queen's palace to the gardens, the formal patterns of hedges, trees and walls, the openings onto the view of the wide Trevisan plain below, and the fountain around which the courtiers

Via Browning, leading up to Piazza Giuseppe Garibaldi in Asolo.

gathered in the shade of the laurels. This idyll no longer exists, and all that remains of the fabled castle are the tower and a single slab of wall. A bar in the garden, selling bottles of Peroni beer and *panini* filled with *prosciutto*, is the sole occupant of the terraces where her courtiers once set themselves literary puzzles and solved etymological riddles. The views still exist though, from this 'town of a hundred horizons', as Gabriele D'Annunzio called it, and you can wander along the parapet of the castle at any time of day and see the countryside Bembo once gazed upon.

The ex-Queen of Cypress, Jerusalem and Armenia is not forgotten today. Her memory is kept alive, and some of her furniture and pictures, as well as her portrait, are vigorously dusted and polished by an eccentric old woman who is keeper of the fifteenth-century Loggia del Capitano, a tiny museum just below the castle, facing the piazza. I spent hours here with this immensely verbose and knowledgeable person, who regards the plump olive-skinned ex-queen as an intimate. How she arranged her hair and who she slept with are related with equal authority, though the sources of her

information about the latter are a mystery. Even the very detailed notes kept by the Venetian secret police in the fifteenth century drew the line at noting down the private details of her various affairs.

The museum also houses some of Eleanora Duse's stage costumes, which hang like shrouds in a cupboard on an upper floor. The great Duse once lived in Asolo (in fact she is buried here as well) and the keeper, equally familiar with the smallest details of *her* life, allowed me to flick through her notebooks and to run my hands through the folds of her clothes. Robert Browning's pens and some of the incidental bric-a-brac of his life at Asolo languish in cases, and if it's your lucky day you can hold them too. The museum's keeper has never been outside a radius of about ten kilometres of Asolo. Perhaps she lives her life through her illustrious charges, who also include the Romans of Asolo and their Neolithic predecessors, whose remaining relics are housed in the basement.

Asolo today is predominantly Renaissance. Partially surrounded by ancient walls, now incorporated into the houses, the main streets, the Via Browning, the Via Roma and the Via Regina Cornaro, are flanked by arcades supported by stout stone piers and lined with shops, a few restaurants and a handful of bars. Beneath the arcades are pink and yellow marble pavements and, above, mullioned and trefoiled windows. Centuries of laden shoppers have staggered through these streets and taken short cuts down small, hidden flights of steps to their homes in tiny ancient cul de sacs. Cars can pass freely through the town, though the one-way system necessitated by the narrowness of the streets makes driving slow and irksome.

In the arcades of the Via Browning are most of the town's vegetable shops and delicatessens. At number 185 is the Enoteca Agnolotti, in whose blackened inner recesses you can buy – and taste – nearly every kind of alcoholic liquid refreshment produced in the hills and on the

An al fresco *pasticceria, Asolo.*

plains of the Veneto. Here, among the cobwebs and the old faithfuls leaning over the bar, grappa is of course the most obvious thing to taste, the variety called Grappa d'Asolo being one of the few that sets your stomach on fire and not your mouth (as with whisky, this is a sign of something rather better than just run of the mill). A rarity, if you can find it, is a wine called Clinton, made from an American grape that survived the phylloxera vine epidemic that over-ran Europe in the nineteenth century.

At number 153 Via Browning it is possible to buy almost any type of pasta, local or otherwise, as well as local wine, cakes, sweets and cooked meats. They also sell here the ingredients for risotto, one of the staples of the Venetian diet. Rice, introduced by the Arabs, grows in vast quantities in the marshlands of the River Po; *risotto al tagio*, with eels and freshwater crayfish, or *risi e bisi*, not actually a risotto but a thick soup, made with rice and peas and flavoured

with onion, ham and celery, are two of the most popular local rice dishes. The shops here also sell five varieties of *radicchio*, a Venetian endive, which is used in risottos, with pasta or in salads; alternatively it can be grilled or fried in olive oil.

These ingredients can also be bought in the weekly vegetable market that takes up most of the Piazza Giuseppe Garibaldi and Piazza Angelo Brugnoli. Mounds of pumpkins, leeks and courgettes are stacked against the fountain and on tables under red canopies, and blood from game and pathetic piles of songbirds trickles between the cracks in the cobbles, mingling with the overspill from the fountain's sprays and turning the floor of the market into a pale red carpet.

Asolo's restaurants are well stocked with the produce of this market: at 11 Piazza D'Annunzio is the Hostaria Ca'Derton and at 85 Via Pietro Bembo, La Papessa, or you can eat at the Hotel Villa Cipriani in the Via Canova. This

A decorative gateway (left); *and antiques in the market overlooked by the church of Santa Maria di Breda in Asolo.*

large house belonged to Robert Browning and contains some of his furniture, as well as other things that were once in Eleanora Duse's house, not far away in the Via Cavour.

Asolo is the best base from which to visit this area of the Veneto. At Conegliano, a few kilometres to the east, is the Cima Foundation, housed in the painter's old house, and the Sala dei Battuti, with magnificent frescoes by Francesco da Milano. And at Castelfranco

Veneto, to the south, is the painter Giorgione's house, with a magnificent *pala* (altarpiece) by this great Venetian artist in the Duomo.

Castelfranco, built on the flat, is a good place for an outing from Asolo. It has one of the best restaurants in the district, the Osteria ai due Mori in the Vicolo Montebelluna, which is very close to the Duomo. The oldest eating establishment in the town, it concentrates on traditional recipes like *pasta e fagioli*, a kind of

The winged lion of St Mark (top left) *a symbol of Venice, and evidence of Feltre's allegiance to it.*
(Bottom left) *A villa on the outskirts of Feltre.*

pasta soup with beans in it, and other oddities called *sopa coada*, *xaeti*, and *pinsa*. You can also eat *prosciutto*, not ham in this case but finely sliced horse meat. About five kilometres outside Asolo is a little town called San Zenone degli Ezzelini, with another excellent restaurant called Ristorante alla Torre, where the specialist dishes contain *porcini* and *chiodini*, two wild, and very expensive, varieties of mushroom.

While much of Catherine Cornaro's gentle idyll still exists in one form or another at Asolo, albeit sometimes streamlined and neatly packaged for passing tourists, Possagno is still rather rough around the edges. It lies at the very edge of the Alpine foothills and overlooks the Venetian plain. Dominating the town, beneath Monte Pallone, is Canova's vast mausoleum, modelled on the Pantheon in Rome. Paintings by Giordano, Palma the Younger and Pordenone decorate the walls, and there are

*F*lowers adorn a handsome building in Feltre.

also works by Canova himself. In the rain this building is imbued with the same icy frigidity as Canova's classically inspired sculptures, some of the working models for which are housed in his old home, now a museum called the Gipsoteca Canoviana. This stands in the town's main square, next to the Cafe Canova where, if you can't be bothered to visit the Gipsoteca, you can always admire Canova's works on the postcards and the little triangular flags on sale. The cafe also does a good line in plastic and plaster reproductions of his *Repentant Magdalen* and a variety of nude Venus and rather coy, naked reclining Adonis.

East of Possagno and Asolo, on the road from Asolo to Crocetta, is the Villa Barbaro (now Volpi) at Maser, one of Palladio's masterpieces, with magnificent frescoes by Veronese. And at Fanzolo, just to the north of Castelfranco, is the Villa Emo, another of Palladio's villas. Both are still private and both are open to the public.

Beyond the Villa Barbaro, the main road, the SS 348, turns northwards to Feltre. Deep in the foothills of the Dolomites, this little town, on a ridge overlooking the indecisive wanderings of the Piave River, is a remarkably homogeneous collection of early sixteenth-century buildings. During the war of the League of Cambrai, Feltre was completely wiped out by the troops of Maximilian as a punishment for its loyalty to Venice, and its citizens were massacred. As a reward for their fidelity, the Venetians rebuilt parts of the town – the church and the principal buildings – and left the citizens to do the rest.

This unbending loyalty to Venice was the result of an agreement reached between the two cities in 1404. Today this union is celebrated with a magnificent *palio*, held in July in the town's old centre. A procession of men and women dressed in fifteenth-century costume moves along the Largo Castaldi to the Via Mezzaterra and then to the Piazza Maggiore, which is enclosed by the castle, the church of San Rocco, the Municipio and the decorative façade of the Palazzo Guarnieri. An archery contest takes place in the Piazza, followed by a display of banner waving. In their period costumes and surrounded by the homogeneous backdrop of the old town, the people of Feltre make the past come alive. Boys still sit on the edge of Tullo Lombardo's fountain (also sixteenth-century) dangling their feet against its venerable edges, shouting at passers-by, jeering or cheering at the procession. Street vendors meander through the crowds as they always have done, selling snacks and drinks, and people hang banners and carpets out of their windows lining the processional route. The whole town unites on this occasion as they did against the imperial troops in the sixteenth century and once again against the Nazis in the Second World War.

Every Friday the itinerant market – the one that camps at Asolo earlier in the week – comes to town. Feltre's Largo Panfilo Castaldi fills up with wagon-loads of vegetables, bucketsful of real and artificial flowers, doormats, corkscrews, dresses, gumboots and huge mobile 'icetrays' full of fresh fish. The vegetables and fruit are stacked in vast quantities on the pavements, along with live rabbits, chickens and ducks which, once you have picked one, are quickly and discreetly knocked over the head and bundled into the shopping bag. The market, which spreads itself out under the chestnuts, beneath the ramparts of the old town, is to some extent the zenith of the housewives' week: cut price articles tempt them away from the shops, and the scent of possible bargains encites them to spend most of their day gossiping over stalls, ever-watchful of price fluctuations.

Belluno, a hill town to the east of Feltre, has a daily market in the Piazza del Mercato. Vegetables (the Veneto is richer in vegetables than any other region of Italy), fish and horsemeat, Asiago and smoked Montasio cheeses, salamis and sausages – *soppressata* and *salsicce all'aglio* –

*T*he works of Morta da Feltre and his pupils adorn
many of the houses of the town.

have been sold here since time immemorial, overlooked by a large Bellini-esque fresco of the Madonna and Child. The lush landscape in the background of the fresco is as much a symbol of the Veneto's fecundity as are the rich varieties and abundance of produce on sale. The arcaded piazza, which is awash with fish scales and lettuce leaves by mid-morning, centres on a fifteenth-century fountain, and is crammed into a tiny space between ancient Venetian gothic houses. Some of these are *trattorie* which open onto the pavements in front: the Cafe Venturato, under the arcade, opens into the market itself and extends a very generous line in credit to the stallholders, fortifying them with wine and beer at increasingly diminishing intervals until, at about 1.00 p.m., everyone totters away and the market closes.

From the Piazza del Mercato, down the Via Realtà to the Via Carrera, is a series of little interconnecting streets and alleyways, a dis-organized jumble of passages, some for pedestrians only, some for cars. This mixture creates a novel form of *passeggiata* at the end of each day. Most people wander backwards and forwards, following the hidden line that directs their feet and guides them past the designer shops and the high profile cafes and bars, in a never-ending perambulation that takes the same route day after day. Others operate an alternative *passeggiata* by car, queueing for hours in organized traffic jams, leaning out of car windows and whistling at friends, music blaring. They park, double park, hoot, drive away, come back – a sequence of events that drowns the passers-by in wholesome blasts of diesel fumes. This *giro* goes round and round until dinnertime, lines of cars following each other nose to tail, along the Via Realtà and the Via Mezza, through the Piazza del Duomo and past the sixteenth-century cathedral, the Museo Civico and Juvarra's belltower, then doubling back to the

Canova's vast mausoleum at Possagno, modelled on the Pantheon in Rome.

Via Carrera and the Piazza Vittorio Emanuele.

Way to the south is Arqua Petrarca, which was an important town in the Middle Ages. Its two brief periods of power, before the fifteenth century, left it with a sprinkling of fine, if rather lowly, ancient buildings that straggle down the sides of one of the 'blue' Euganean hills. These brief interludes were unique in Arqua's history and, once over, the town slipped into a state of lethargy and poverty. This preserved its character, and Arqua today is consistently medieval in appearance.

Not much has changed here since the poet Petrarch arrived in 1370, taking over a house at the top of the town, in a position chosen for its distant views. This building survives, and is naturally the principal goal of any passing visitor to Arqua. Set behind a high brick wall, it has an ancient core and some sixteenth-century modifications. Today it is open to the public, and in it can be seen traces of frescoes portraying Laura, the young girl with whom Petrarch fell in love. A spectacular medieval seat occupies one room of the house and is said to be the poet's own, though this is open to speculation. There are other miscellaneous bits and pieces associated with his life, and there is a visitor's book signed by, among others, Byron and his mistress, Teresa Guiccioli.

Outside the walls of Petrarch's garden, the other little cottages lining the streets remain much as he would have known them. Not far from his house is the once roofed fourteenth-century loggia of the 'Vicari', who governed the town for the Venetians, and the small church of the Trinità, with its high altar surmounted by a painting by Palma il Giovane. Lower down the town, in the Via alla Piazza, is the Taverna di Laura, facing an open space containing Petrarch's sarcophagus.

Although Petrarch found Arqua a beautiful, peaceful retreat, a restorative for his rather wearied soul, when he moved there four years before his death, he was aware of the violent characteristics of its inhabitants. He remarked on their tendency to seek peace of mind in alcoholic oblivion, calling them 'a drunkard people for whom life is not in blood but in wine'. Until modernization of the road network in the area, and the opening up of the town in the 1960s, much of the inhabitants' medieval ferocity remained. They maintained no relations with their neighbours whom, it has been said, 'they greet first with stones, then with knives'. One recent incident is remembered when an Arquain, on the way to Padua by bus, had to get off en route because he felt uncomfortable going to the city without the pruning knife he always carried in his hip pocket, and which he had forgotten when getting into his Sunday suit.

Even as late as 1966 much of Arqua was a squalid ruin, and it is still relatively difficult to get to. Byron and his mistress had to walk there because their coach couldn't manage the steep roads and the bumpy terrain. Life is a little less arduous nowadays; trains can get within four kilometres of the town (the nearest railway station is at Monselice), and it is only a few kilometres off the main Rovigo–Padua road, the SS 16.

Evidence of Feltre's allegiances to Venice are seen in the architectural style of the town.

LOMBARDY

NESSO · CIVENNA · BERGAMO

Most of Lombardy is a flat plain, immensely fertile, well populated and industrialized. If you can drag yourself away from hazy beauty of the pale wheat and rice fields, the canals and the lines of poplars, the scenic routes north of Milan are many and varied. Between Milan and the northern Alps are the great lakes, Maggiore, Lugano, Como and Garda, as well as two smaller ones, Orta and Iseo. The roughest and most spectacular country borders on Switzerland. Up here the valleys below the peaks of the Alpi Orbie are like fissures in walls of solid rock. Good for skiing, good for climbing, these areas are sparsely populated. The communities that do exist here are inevitably an ethnic mix reflecting centuries of fluctuating border lines. Variety in terms of language, architecture, cooking and even, to some extent, the physical appearance of the people, is the norm.

By contrast, the hills climbing out of the lakes are dotted with towns. Many of them are now smudged together, indistinguishable from their neighbours. But some, like Nesso on the banks of Lake Como, just north of the town of Como, can't expand in any direction because of the sheet of water in front and the steep slopes of Monte Primo behind. Almost hidden as you approach from Lezzeno, further north, Nesso springs suddenly into view on the hillside running down to the water's edge. It is actually built in two distinct sections, which may at one time have been two villages. Further along the road is the second and liveliest part of it, which includes the remains of a Sforza castle destroyed in the sixteenth century. The road approaching Nesso is level with the highest point of the church steeple and the worn brown roof tiles and chimney stacks of the little houses. It is a town to be avoided if all you have with you are your sling-backs. The forces of gravity will overcome them as you attempt the descent into the inner recesses of the town, and you'll end up with a broken ankle.

What you will miss is the kind of view that enchanted Pliny, who had several villas on the lake's shore. On a good day there is nothing more lyrically serene than the sight of the opposite bank of the lake reflected in the sheen on Como's placid water. If you follow the main passageway through the town, tripping over the huge uneven cobbles, past the spectral gloom of

Bergamo (above) rises out of the Lombardy plain just at the foothills of the Alps. (Right) Detail of the Biblioteca Civica, modelled in Sansovino's library building in Venice. (Overleaf) Detail of the crazy entrance façade of the Colleoni chapel, built to commemorate a successful mercenary.

old doorways and the crevices between the buildings, you will eventually come to a narrow stone landing stage which juts out into the water under the overhanging wisteria. An afternoon here with some *panini* (filled rolls) from the bar, and a bottle of something, provided you've remembered to bring the corkscrew, is as pleasant a way as any to view the lake.

An air of melancholy hangs over Nesso. Although its cafes and bars are lively and noisy, the minute you enter some darkened back alley or walk into the lower town, too small for traffic, Nesso is silent. Memories of the Inquisition are never far away; all those poor souls dragged screaming from their houses by the henchmen of San Carlo Borromeo in the sixteenth century, destined for the pyres in the *piazze* of Milan and Como, have left a sad taint on the place. San Carlo was aiming to drive the devil out of the people of Nesso and nearby Lezzeno, and ever

The Palazzo della Ragione in Bergamo.

more appalling tortures were inflicted on them in an effort to make them toe the line. It isn't really surprising that people confessed to crimes they never committed when seated naked on a red hot bronze horse, or when parts of their bodies were roasted slowly over a fire. Who wouldn't beg to have the devil exorcized from their body when their limbs were being smashed to pieces and then fed through the spokes of a turning wheel?

The bells of the parish church of SS Pietro e Paolo, which once tolled for the slaughtered citizens of Nesso, now only toll the hour. But there are happier places along the Como coastline. Civenna, for example, is one, way above the eastern leg of the lake, and Torno, just south of Nesso, is another. Here the church of San Giovanni Battista contains one of the nails, supposedly, from the Cross. Legend has it that it was left here by a bishop returning home

The Contarini Fountain in the middle of
Piazza Vecchia, Bergamo.

after a successful crusade in the Holy Land. He was washed ashore in a storm and, believing this to be a sign from God, allowed the relic to remain on the spot. He also carried a leg bone belonging to some other worthy; this he also left behind when he departed.

But perhaps the most interesting hill town in Lombardy is one that lies nowhere near the major lakes. This is Bergamo, which rises out of the Lombardy plain just at the foothills of the Alps, thirty kilometres along the A4, north-east of Milan. Frank Lloyd Wright came here and pronounced it a wonderful town, which 'stuns the man who is approaching it'.

This is true if you see Bergamo early in the morning, while the mists still cover both the plain around it and the flat *città bassa*, the lower town, at its foot, and all that is visible are the silhouettes of the domes, towers and belfries of the *città alta*, high on its hill. They rise above the plain like a ghostly mirage in a frozen desert. Most people who come to Bergamo are enchanted by its picturesque qualities. Stendhal couldn't believe that the view he was contemplating over the parapets of the upper town's walls was so enchanting; Montanelli practically wept as he compared the perfection of Bergamo to Siena, which he claimed had few rivals. You must decide for yourself. Bergamo in the winter has a glacial clarity which is, without doubt, enchanting if you're wearing thick gloves and thermal underwear. In the summer it takes on one or two distinctly Mediterranean characteristics, and the Duomo, like all Italian duomos, with their inherent dankness, is a relief to boiled travellers, who jostle with each other to ease their sunburnt flesh against the cold marble slabs of its interior.

The lower town has long straight streets and arcades of shops and cafes. The main thoroughfare, the Sentierone, is where the people of Bergamo *fanno lo struscio*, exhibit themselves and their finery. The Sentierone is not unlike a cat-walk and, perhaps because of

Domes and belfries of the città alta, Bergamo.

the proximity to Milan, the *passeggiata* here proceeds like a fashion show. Up and down the Bergamascans stroll, self-conscious, watchful, comparing fashion notes, and now and again dipping into a bar for a quick *caffè* before resuming their endless promenade. In the winter the women are shameless in thick fur coats, and in the summer nearly naked in body-hugging two-piece outfits. Bronzed and taut, they are the very best advertisements for the fashion industry. The only concession Italian men make to the heat is to dispense with socks, so that their brown feet contrast with their black or brown leather moccasins.

The *città bassa* has a number of *palazzi*, churches (including San Bartolomeo, with its sixteenth-century altarpiece by Lorenzo Lotto) and of course the municipal art gallery, the Accademia Pinacoteca Carrara, which houses a wide-ranging collection of art from the Venetian, Lombard and Tuscan schools as well as important works by painters such as Rubens,

Raphael and Van Dyck. There is also a theatre dedicated to Gaetano Donizetti.

The upper town has none of the nineteenth-century regimentation of the lower. Up here you still have to enter via the narrowest of apertures in the city walls, one car at a time. It is an enchanting place, with gardens, courtyards and old cobbled streets. The Piazza Vecchia is the heart of the old town, which all the ancient maze-like streets around it strive to gain access to. It is completely enclosed by a range of *palazzi*, some of which are medieval; others, like the Biblioteca Civica, which is modelled on Sansovino's library in Venice, date from the sixteenth century.

Behind the Piazza Vecchia are the Duomo and the fifteenth-century Cappella Colleoni. The extraordinarily ornate façade of the Cappella speaks volumes about the pretensions of the man whose tomb lies inside it. Bartolomeo Colleoni who, apart from Donizetti, is Bergamo's most famous son, was a *condottiere* of

The south portal of the Basilica of Santa Maria Maggiore.

the first league. Along with the likes of Gat-temelata, Bande Nere and Sir John Hawkwood, he terrorized a variety of city states, selling him-self and his prowess with the sword to the highest bidder. He made a fortune, and this chapel is his monument to posterity.

Discerning art historians laugh at this Cap-pella, a ridiculous artifice of classicism laid over a gauche Renaissance-style lump of a building. But I couldn't help but stop and stare at its dif-ferent coloured marbles and its frenetic external decoration, which includes busts, statues, bas reliefs and a central rose window. Within is a dyspeptic, rather wooden Colleoni, astride a golden horse which has seen better days and which seems to have a bad dose of arthritis. Nonetheless, the interior is magnificent and even Tiepolo was persuaded to carry out some of its decoration. Attached to one side of the Duomo (the vestry was pulled down to make way for this chapel) it has a pride of place that its patron certainly did not deserve.

The Piazza Vecchia is the focus of the *passeg-giata* both at lunch-time and in the evenings. Passing it at one end is the Via Colleoni, which leads down through the town and eventually becomes the Via Gombito. Around the piazza and in this long thoroughfare are the upper town's shops, bars and cafes, and the babbling populace keeps strictly to this area when strol-ling, perhaps because the *passeggiata* is all the more rewarding if you can catch sight of your-

self in a large plate-glass shop window – and there are many in this part of town. Here you can allow yourself a surreptitious glance at your reflection and make minor adjustments. Reas-sured, with confidence duly restored, who knows, you might pick up the stranger of your dreams – and all Bergamo is here, students, fashion plates, gracious old women in black with patent leather shoes and the odd sprinkling of old men in grey hats.

Bergamo is a good place to indulge in a little of the region's cuisine. Choose the Ristorante Sole, near the Piazza Vecchia, in the Via Col-leoni, or the Trattoria del Sommelier in the Via Fara, near the entrance to the *città alta*. Bergamascan food is more Venetian than any-thing else, Bergamo having once been a part of the Venetian Republic, and fish is always high on the better menus. There is actually an excel-lent fish market here, which seems strange con-sidering that the nearest stretch of water is about seventy kilometres away, at Lake Iseo. Polenta, a porridge like substance which some people like, and which sticks to the top of your mouth, is common in this region. In fact it was the staple of the rural poor until the Thirties. Made with water or milk mixed with grain, it is served with beans or vegetables, hot, cold, sli-ced, fried or grilled. You can even have it top-ped with skewers of small birds: *polenta e osei* is a speciality of Bergamo, sold by all the local restaurants.

The cafés spill out into the Piazza Vecchia in Bergamo (left). At the heart of Bergamo's città alta (above), the Piazza Vecchia is dominated on one side by the façade of the Biblioteca Civica, the civic library.

LIGURIA

BAIARDO · BUSSANA VECCHIA · DOLCEACQUA
APRICALE · TRIORA

Catastrophes of all descriptions, manmade and natural, have always been fairly common in Liguria. In this narrow, mountainous region of north-west Italy – where the ravines and peaks of the Maritime Alps abruptly vanish and reappear behind other jagged mountain ranges – earthquakes, cholera, brutal pirate raids and oppressive rule by feudal barons battered the hill towns into their present shape, and contributed to the Ligurians' remarkable resilience in times of stress and extreme pressure. For this they are still much admired.

The interior of Liguria is strangely different from its coastline. The important trees here are not the myrtles, oleanders and palms of the fashionable Riviera. What matters in the mountains are the figs, olives, chestnuts and vines which, in times of hardship, would form the basis of a subsistence diet.

Liguria has none of the gently undulating countryside of Tuscany or Umbria. Instead, it is a landscape of steep inclines, where the recesses of the narrow valleys are almost permanently dark from lack of sunshine. Where plants and trees haven't been coaxed out of an unyielding,

stony ground there are only scraggy pines and scrub. Strewn along the upper reaches of these barren valleys are the hill towns, which are still among the most evocatively feudal in northern Italy. Seen from below, they appear abandoned, their windows gaping; half fortress, half town, the houses, church and rock are welded together, dank, cobbled and ramshackle.

In the nineteenth century, travellers approached the ancient Ligurian hill towns with caution. It's not that they were unsafe; as Augustus Hare put it, they were not 'civilized'. One traveller felt that the hill towns on the way south through Liguria, to Genoa and Pisa, were seen 'to greater advantage in distant view than in close approach to them. A poetical contemplation, that might have been lulled with romantic wanderings only a few months before, must wake up in fright on finding itself ... confined to the minutiae of one of these filthy places ...'. The squalor experienced by this traveller is not hard to imagine. Many of the places he spoke of with such derision survive, though relative prosperity, or else utter ruin and decay, have replaced the squalor. At the top end of Baiardo, for

Triora (above) is a fortified town – half fortress, half town – where the houses, churches and rock are welded together, dark, cobbled and ramshackle. (Right) From the side of Monte Trono there is almost an 360-degree view of the surrounding countryside.

example, a hill town near San Remo in western Liguria, some of the houses are still shared with chickens and sheep, and some of the narrow paved streets and alleys, particularly those tunnelled under the buildings, have never been washed down by the rain or seen the sunlight. In the *città bassa* at Triora, further inland from Baiardo, some of the houses are occupied by goats, and the alleys are awash with droppings and straw.

In 1887 an earthquake, one of many since they were first recorded in western Liguria in 1222, brought down the roof of the church of San Nicola at Baiardo, killing most of the worshippers. It was Ash Wednesday and the church was full. Barely ten kilometres away, Bussana Vecchia was wrecked, though only 53 of its 800 inhabitants lost their lives. But Ceriana, a fortified hill town between the two, surrounded by pines, olives and chestnuts, barely felt the tremors. Recovering, the people of Baiardo simply transferred the centre of their religious activity to the romanesque church of San Gregorio down the hill, and San Nicola was abandoned to the weeds and left to rot. It is still crumbling away, its frescoes fading in the sunlight and the rain.

But this was just another calamity in an already turbulent history. Other, more

In the gloom (above) *lurk the ghosts of past atrocities, not least of which was the burning of a 'witch'.* (Right) *In contrast, one of the many saints revered in Triora.*

wretched, events had dogged the hill towns of Liguria over the centuries. The Romans were pushed out of the Italian peninsula by the invasion of the Goths, the Longobards and then the Franks. Since the natural approach to this narrow region, squeezed between the water and Piedmont, is from the sea, Liguria was also terrorized by Saracen pirates. Their lightning raids carried off the women and children of nearly all the west Ligurian hill towns within easy reach of the coast – Ceriana, Baiardo, Dolceacqua, Apricale, Pigna and even Triora, nearly thirty kilometres inland. In the tenth century the Saracens murdered most of the inhabitants of Bussana and destroyed their town, which at that time lay lower down in the valley. The survivors of the raid simply moved to the top of the hill, about 200 metres above sea level, and built a new town in a situation that they could better defend under attack. From Castello di Bussana, the new, medieval Bussana (which was destroyed by the earthquake of 1887) they had an excellent view of the sea.

Following the earthquake, yet another Bussana was built further down the same hill, and officially the medieval town ceased to exist; from afar it has the look of a sun-dried skeleton.

S. AGOSTINO

Unofficially, however, the remains of this medieval hulk have been wired up with telephone and electricity cables, and it is now home to a very obscure colony of German artists and craftsmen whose studios line the main street, the Via degli Archi, below the shattered broken church.

Perhaps the grimmest years in the history of Liguria were those of the Middle Ages, when the oppressive rule of the feudal barons preyed on every aspect of the peasants' daily lives. Neighbouring overlords murdered each other and their respective vassals, destroyed each other's crops, looted the churches, raped the women and drove off the cattle. It is not surprising that with such instability Liguria never produced any early patrons of the arts, or showed any great flowering of painting, sculpture or architecture.

Guarding the entrance to the Nervia River valley, between Ventimiglia and San Remo, and about seven kilometres from the coast, is Dolceacqua. This rock town, with a castle at its summit, was the principal stronghold of a branch of the Doria clan, forebears of the great Genoese admiral Andrea Doria, from the thirteenth to the eighteenth centuries. Butting against its ramparts, and lining steep, narrow alleyways and long flights of steps, are blackened stone houses redolent of watchfulness, insecurity and suspicion. With their small narrow windows and long dark shadows, they have a grim but compelling appeal.

No building in Dolceacqua has been altered quite as many times as the castle, the nucleus of which dates from the twelfth century. Other bits were built two hundred years later, and the entire structure was enriched and embellished in the late fifteenth century, giving it a palatial veneer which hid the reality of the fortress within. It was partly destroyed by the 'modern' artillery fire of a Franco-Spanish army in 1746,

The church of San Nicola, at the highest point of Baiardo, was destroyed in an earthquake so the villagers moved the sacrament to another church, San Gregorio, lower down the hill.

in the Austrian War of Succession, and after that the Doria family moved into the Palazzo Doria further down the town, alongside the church of Sant'Antonio Abate.

Although the castle was virtually impenetrable, its owners never ruled out the possibility of a conqueror gaining access to it. They dug an escape tunnel out of the rock, down the south side of the castle, to the river which runs through the middle of the town below; part of this tunnel is still visible in the Cantina di Luigi Mauro detto Lui, in the piazza in front of the church. There are supposed to be two other tunnels, one running under the river bed to connect the castle with the opposite bank, and another from the Piazza della Canonica to the church of San Giorgio, nearly two kilometres away. However, these two have become part of local folklore and no trace of either has ever been found.

The rhythm of daily life at Dolceacqua is slow and easy. Men fish in the river in the centre of the town, and each week, at a specified hour, the women can be seen carrying large

*T*riora was once an extremely powerful stronghold that presented a considerable threat to the security of the territories of the Republic of Genoa.

baking tins on their heads to the *forno*, the bakery, in the Borgo, the quarter surrounding the castle. This peculiarly Brueghelesque procession wends its way there through the old worn passages and alleys, each participant a perfect example of rustic femininity, clad in black cardigan and stout country boots. Everyone here adheres to the invariable pattern of country life, whose gentle existence today belies the town's sinister past.

Dolceacqua was most probably a Druidic site at one time. Contrary to common belief, the derivation of its name is nothing like its lyrical English translation of 'sweet water'; instead it derives from the name of Dus, the mysterious sorceress (called Sagana in Celtic), who lived in a cave on nearby Monte Abellio with a soothsayer called Hairolo and other Druids. From Dus and Sagana, to Dussaga, to Dulcisaqua in the thirteenth century, it finally became Dolceacqua. If this was a sacred site, it would have been the Galli Nervi, a Celtic tribe, who revered it and who used to placate the gods on the banks of the Nervia River with offerings of

Brightly painted houses and churches at the centre of the town of Pigna which is one of the more picturesque towns in Liguria.

the blood of small children.

Much later the site became the scene of even more barbarous activity under the Doria clan. A ghost, thought to be that of a girl called Lucrezia, haunts the ramparts of the castle annually in the early days of August. Lucrezia was the victim of Imperiale Doria's revival of the ancient right of *jus primae noctis*, which had been abolished by his grandfather in 1250. This entitled the lordling to spend the night with the bride of any of his vassals on the eve of her wedding. Imperiale, finding that Lucrezia refused to succumb without a fight, threw her into a dungeon, where she died of starvation. The townspeople were so enraged by this animal behaviour that they seized Imperiale in his own bed and, under pain of death, marched him to Genoa, where the Doge, to whom he owed allegiance, made him sign a statement relinquishing his right. On his return to Dolceacqua the women of the town presented him with little cakes called *michete*, made of flour, eggs, sugar and lemon peel – sweet compensation for his loss.

This event is commemorated annually on 15 August, when the Dolceacqua youths swagger through the alleys and passages of the town crying '*a micheta, donne*'. The girls open the windows and shower them with the little cakes, taking care to aim them at their own particular lovers. The irony of this is not lost on an outside observer; the women of Dolceacqua once had to keep not only an arrogant feudal baron in check but also (as now) their own men, whose passions had a tendency to explode from time to time.

Dolceacqua produces a red wine called the Rossese di Dolceacqua. Ever since 1796, when the young Napoleon came here as a guest of the Marchesa Teresina Doria and took a fancy to the wine, it has been the staple of Dolceacqua's economy. It can be tasted in the *cantine* of the Via Doria, behind the Piazza Padre Giovanni Mauro, or others on the steep path that leads up to the castle. Follow the signs.

Apricale was another Doria fiefdom in the Nervia valley, a few kilometres up-river from Dolceacqua. It is by far the most striking of the rock towns of the district. It looks as if God might have poured it down the side of the hill and, like Dolceacqua, it is struggling to prevent itself from falling into the river below. The muddle of houses, so tightly crammed around its castle that it is difficult to distinguish one from the other, are a strange mixture of buildings. Some are part empty, decaying and shattered, while others are restored and inhabited.

Today Apricale is a benign little place, resounding with children's yells, church bells tolling the hour, dogs barking and birdsong. Stray cats lie about in empty stone washbasins in the ancient public laundry area (old stone sinks in a row with a single tap and a trough for water behind), and old women drag out their seats and sit in the main piazza to sun themselves and pass the time of day. This is a secluded world, which neither cars nor buses can enter because the streets are too narrow. Only a steep and tortuous climb through cobbled, tunnel-like alleys and passageways on foot

The tiny covered lanes of Triora are part deserted, part restored.

will take you to the centre. The principal shops are all there – one butcher, one grocer, one hairdresser – but they are easily missed because they don't advertise their presence.

Some of these Ligurian hill towns have nothing more than an interesting festival to offer the traveller. Baiardo has its Festa della Barca, a strangely pagan ceremony – perhaps originally a fertility rite – which is a very rare survival. On Whitsunday everybody joins hands and dances around a tall pine trunk placed in a hole in the town's central piazza, outside the church. They sing a song whose words tell the story of Angelina, the unfortunate third daughter of Count Rubino of Baiardo, who fell in love with a Saracen sailor whom she had seen felling trees in a nearby wood. Having succumbed to his lusty and unrestrained desires, Angelina tried to follow him after he and his party had departed. Her father, horrified, felt compelled to avenge his family's honour which, because the Saracens were so hated in Liguria, had suffered a considerable blow. He caught up with Angelina and chopped off her head. Today the phallic potential of the felled tree and the dance around it are the lasting reminders of Angelina's dire predicament and the tragedy of her story.

A religious festival held at Triora, a fortified town high on the slopes of Monte Trono, at the head of the neighbouring Val d'Argentina, is much more complex. It was originally celebrated in three localities outside the town, one of which is now abandoned. The main protagonists, dressed in white, are the *Bianchi*, members of the Guild of San Giovanni Battista (Triora's patron saint, called San Zane in the local dialect). On the evening of 23 June each year they carry a heavy life-size wooden statue of the saint (made by Maragliano in the late seventeenth century) from its resting place in the Oratory of San Giovanni, in Piazza Collegiata, to the Sanctuary of San Bernardino, just below the steeply winding approach road to the town. Early the following day, a smaller statue of the saint, called the *piccola*, is then taken, garlanded, on the shoulders of the *Bianchi*, who run with it to the Sanctuary of San Zane. This is no mean feat because the second sanctuary is three hours away, nearly 1500 metres up, on the summit of Monte Ceppo, way above Triora, on the other side of the River Argentina. Other processions from Corte and Andagna, villages in the surrounding hills, join the main procession, *Bianchi* as well as pilgrims, which then goes into San Zane's sanctuary to hear mass.

At San Zane the real festivities begin. While the mass is being said a group of pilgrims, mostly women, walk arm in arm nine times around the sanctuary saying a novena. Each time they pass the door of the building they genuflect. While a buzz of prayer can be heard from them, under the chestnuts raucous boys and old men in hats drink the local rossese or ormeasco wine and eat *torta di riso* (rice cakes) and *cipolle ripiene* (stuffed onions), which are specially reserved for this occasion. The porters of the *piccola* have special treatment; they sit at trestle tables set apart for them under the trees.

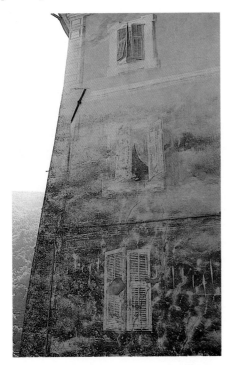

*F*aux *windows on a building at Pighna* (left). (Overleaf) *Great sweeps of countryside, as well as Andagna, can be seen from the windows of Triora.*

By dusk groups of men and women are lying about under the trees in the long grass, dozing in their Sunday finery, handkerchiefs on their heads, their faces glowing from the sun, the wine, the fresh mountain air and contentment. This is probably the longest holiday in their calendar, and the only time that these hard-working mountain communities ever get together to fraternize. The last stage of this *festa* is to return the *piccola* to San Bernardino, this time carried by a single porter. From there Maragliana's San Giovanni is taken back to its sanctuary in the heart of Triora.

Triora was once an extremely powerful stronghold, with its own statutes and civil laws. In its heyday, in the thirteenth century, its belli-cose population, behind their impenetrable walls, could have defended themselves from any one of the five towers of its castle. Perched strategically on the side of Monte Trono, with

From the side of Monte Trono there is a vast panoramic view of the surrounding countryside.

an almost 360-degree view of the surrounding countryside, it presented a considerable threat to the security of the territories of the Republic of Genoa. Once Triora's territories included similar hilltop communities nearby, like Castelvittorio, Ceriana, Montalto, Baiardo and Badalucco (all of which are worth a visit), but at the end of the thirteenth century Genoa finally took Triora. The ensuing peaceful period saw the construction and decoration of its churches, and it was during this lull that the town also acquired its beautiful carved door lintels, such as the Annunciation panel in the Via Sambughea, and others in the Piazza Collegiata and the streets opening off it.

Nowadays Triora is fairly silent. Old Triorese totter down its dark lanes and alleyways, leading goats or pushing barrows overloaded with hay or logs. Wander down the Corso Italia, past the Trattoria/Bar La Tavernetta and into the Quartiere della Sambughea, and you will find yourself in a part of town that is still genuinely and predominently medieval. Here in the gloom of the tunnel-like passages and ancient doorways, are the ghosts of the cholera epidemics, of the Saracen raiders and their victims, of the witch killed in 1588 for having 'connived with the devil' to bring about the devastating drought and famine of 1587, and of the partisans from the surrounding mountains murdered by the Nazis during the Second World War. In the winter nothing stirs down here, in the *città bassa*, except for goats and sheep stabled in deserted rooms and cellars. The only smells are from the woodsmoke of domestic fires and the livestock, and almost the only noise is the distant clanking of saucepans. Water drips into old disused stone sinks from the huge medieval cistern under Piazza Collegiata, once capable of holding enough water to last for several months in the event of a siege.

Though parts of Triora are now empty and forgotten, the town continues to expand. The Corso Italia at its highest point, where it extends beyond the limits of the old town, up among the chestnuts, now has rows of new houses, grandly called *palazzine*, and little flats. Here lies evidence in bricks and mortar of the truth of a statement I found carved in stone on an old garden wall at the bottom of the Vico Ciappa, in the Quartiere della Sambughea, where the Via Camurata turns downhill into Via Sambughea. It says, '*L'agricoltura è la prima base d'ogni richezza*' which, roughly translated, means 'agriculture is the base of all riches'. If you did really well in these self-sufficient hilltop communities, you could prosper and move on, and very likely end up in a new house in the Corso Italia. Fixed on a wall in this same garden in the Vico Ciappa is another sign which says, '*Già abitato da 7 famiglie, oggi, 1935, da una sola*', meaning that the little house was 'Formerly lived in by seven families but today, 1935, by only one'. This ancient little dwelling looking into the fruit trees has been abandoned in favour of the modern luxuries of twentieth-century living.

A damp wintry day in Triora is best ended at La Tavernetta, where tea is made by boiling water on an old cast-iron stove which stands on legs in the corner. Your cappucino or espresso, enjoyed while the locals drink their early morning glass of rossese, would however be made in the conventional fashion. Food, available at lunch-times only, would most probably be prepared according to traditional Ligurian recipes, and consist of *cucina povera*, simple, traditional peasant dishes, using whatever is to hand locally and in season at the time. There might be rabbit or lamb, though generally Ligurian cooking makes little use of red meat, *torta di verdure* (greenery and herbs cooked in a sort of pancake), *trenette verdi* (a ribbon-like pasta served with *pesto*, the basil sauce which is a Ligurian invention), *ravioli* (also reputed to have been born in Liguria) stuffed with offal and herbs from the mountainside, and possibly even fish, mostly *sgombro* (mackerel) and *acciughe* (anchovies).

PIEDMONT

EXILLES · LA MORRA · BAROLO
RODDI D'ALBA · MONCALVO

The Piemontese landscape varies considerably from its northern to its southern extremity. An arc of mountains sweeps round its western boundaries with France and Switzerland, while in the east a plain opens out to Lombardy. The hill towns of the north – Exilles and Gravere, for example, at the end of the Monginevro Pass – are completely different from those of the south-east, in the Langhe district and the Monferrato hills. Exilles, up near Susa, west of Turin, balances on a ledge on the side of a mountain above the River Bardonecchia, and seems to grow out of the stony terrain around it. Those of south-eastern Piedmont are generally perched on the highest points of the gently undulating hills.

If you enter Italy from France, via the Monginevro Pass, you could well be following in the footsteps of Hannibal, with his army of nearly 30,000 Carthaginians and their herd of elephants. This spectacular entourage crossed the Alps into the Italian peninsula in order to confront the Romans on their home territory. Their exact route history doesn't specify. It only speculates. Ancient sources, like Polibius, mention a route along the Isere, through the Little St Bernard Pass, though at the time it would have been peopled by some particularly unpleasant warlike tribes. Livy argues the case for the Monginevro Pass, which approaches the town of Susa from the west, a route well known in Hannibal's time and well used since, possibly because it was the easiest. Other, later, theories favour the Moncinesio, though it was little known at the time, while the Great St Bernard was too narrow, high and steep, and the Carthaginian army would have had to have been acrobats to have crossed by that route.

Livy was most probably right. The Monginevro Pass, having wound its way down the Col di Monginevro, enters the Susa valley way above Exilles, a place with a grim fascination. As a frontier town, it had to guard what became one of the most important routes into Italy, and was used by conquerors from Charlemagne to Napoleon. A few hundred yards from Exilles, on a rock in the middle of the Susa valley, is an iron-grey fortress, one of the grimmest, most forbidding strongholds ever constructed. Built in the seventeenth century,

A typical sight (above) *encountered on any Italian road.* (Right) *The vegetable market in Piazza Garibaldi, Moncalvo.*

178

dismantled in 1796 and reconstructed twenty years later according to its original plan, it became a French state prison after France invaded the valley in 1630. It was during this period that the Man in the Iron Mask was incarcerated here. One day, it is said, a shadowy figure, heavily guarded and completely covered in a waxed linen shroud, with openings only for eyes and mouth, was taken north through the town, carried on a litter by eight porters from the castle. Whether or not this was the Man in the Iron Mask being moved to Paris – where, according to French records, he died in the Bastille in 1703 – is uncertain; the people of Exilles maintain that he is buried in their parish church, but no recognizable tomb has ever been discovered there. The truth behind this story, or legend, is as impenetrable as the fortress is today. The sad prisoner, whom Voltaire believed to have been the twin brother of Louis

Decorations for a festa, Moncalvo.

XIV of France, came to Exilles with his gaoler, Sarit Mars, one of the original Three Musketeers, from Pinerolo, another fortress town south-west of Turin. Mars, Governor of Pinerolo, on leaving that post to take up the governorship of Exilles, took his most secret prisoner with him.

The Via Roma, which today runs through the centre of Exilles, with its quiet shops and stone benches in the sun, would once have been part of the main route down the mountain; the people of the town would have been busily engaged in innkeeping and providing meals for weary travellers, some of whom would have arrived on mules or, in the winter, on sledges. On one occasion in the seventeenth century the Duchess of Savoy and her maids shot suddenly into view on the back of an ox hide, pushed from the top of a nearby slope by a porter; the hair on the underside of the hide would have

A rather individual house on the outskirts of La Morra (top right). This hill town is at the centre of the Langhe's viticultural activity (bottom right).

acted as a brake. Nothing as dramatic takes place now as trans-European juggernauts and a constant flow of cars file down into the valley, pausing briefly to glance at the fortress.

Further down the valley is Gravere, another smallish town above the River Bardonecchia. The pass divides the town in two. In the older half, crouching beneath a rock face, are little ancient houses with heavily overhanging eaves and carved balconies and terraces. Virtually every one of them has been abandoned. The newer half of Gravere, built on the considerable profits of flourishing apple and pear orchards nearby, is of little interest.

The most characterful hill towns of Piedmont are those of the Langhe and the Monferrato districts. Much more fertile than the northern valleys, the gentle slopes south-east of Turin were often the incentive as well as the prize for making the arduous and often terrifying Alpine crossing. La Morra, Barolo, Roddi d'Alba and Serralunga d'Alba, south of Alba, are the most important towns of the Langhe, while north of Asti, in Monferrato, Moncalvo and Montiglio are worth a visit. The lifestyle in these towns is extremely rural, the main preoccupation of the inhabitants being viticulture. Each town has a number of small localized festivals or fairs, usually concerned with things edible or drinkable – truffles, snails, grapes or wine. Mainly because of the frequent mists and rain, and the damp cold in winter, the thickly verdant arcadian landscapes of these districts are unfrequented by outsiders other than those in search of a gastronomic treat.

The typical hill towns of the Langhe are clusters of yellow-gold stone houses grouped around a fortress, or, in the case of Serralunga d'Alba, arranged in concentric circles around it. They can be seen from miles away, silhouetted against the sky, dark purple against the sunset and lit by the first rays of morning light. La Morra, which rests on a high, flat-topped hill, is known as the Belvedere of the Langhe. From

Piazza Belvedere, in the shade of the chestnuts of the Ristorante Belvedere, you can look down across the vineyards covering the steep, regular hills of the surrounding landscape. Beyond, on a clear day, or early in the morning, you can see the chain of Alpine peaks encircling Piedmont in the west.

La Morra is spread about on either side of narrow lanes which climb gently up towards the church of San Martino, in Piazza Municipio, and the nearby remains of the castle, destroyed by the French in 1542. Great architecture and great art have no part to play in the daily life of the town but its main monuments, in particular the churches of San Martino and San Rocco, are fairly typical of the area, being built of small orange bricks.

La Morra is at the centre of the Langhe's viticulture. It always has been. As early as 1402 the Nebbiolo grape was used here to produce 'Nebbiolum' wine. Today this grape is the basis for Piedmont's status as the leading wine-producing area in Italy with thirty-seven DOC or DOCG zones (name of origin controlled and name of origin controlled and guaranteed respectively). Around La Morra 436 hectares of land have been allotted to Nebbiolo vines for

The red roofs of La Morra (left), *Barolo* (right), *like most of the towns in the Langhe, is littered with* cantine.

Barolo wine production of DOC status. The Nebbiolo grapes are not harvested until at least mid-October, the period of the Langhe's well-known affliction, the fog, *la nebbia* (possibly the origin of the grape's name). To compensate, the grapes need all the sunshine they can get, so the vines are generally grown on the south sides of the intensely cultivated hills.

In the town itself, where the Piazza Vittorio Emanuele II meets the Via Roma, I found the Vinbar, the pivotal point around which life revolves in this small community. Here the old men of La Morra sit out the empty hours of the *dopopranzo* (after lunch) period, chatting and drinking espresso. These ancient craggy farm-workers, their brows as deeply furrowed as their ploughed autumn fields, are proud of their participation in the production of some of Italy's finest red wines. A gaudy engraved mirror on the wall lists with pride the DOC and DOCG wines of the district. The barman will happily give directions to any one of the five 'wine paths' laid out through the local vineyards, or to one of the town's many wine sellers and *enoteche* (where wines are displayed, tasted and sold).

At number 2 Via Carlo Alberto is the Can-

Houses of unprepossessing appearance line the streets of La Morra which is known as the 'Belvedere of the Langhe' (above). La Morra (right).

tina di La Morra, which acts as agent and wholesaler for the various local wine producers where, at specified hours, wines are laid out for tasting. There are others: the Cantina dj'Amis, in the Via Vittorio Emanuele II, and the Cantina Vinicola Piemontese, in the Strada del Langhetto. Generally these deal in Barolo wine, though they also sell Dolcetto d'Alba, Barbera d'Alba and Nebbiolo d'Alba.

The pursuit of viticulture is never, it seems, allowed to take precedence over religious activity. This I discovered, much to my annoyance, when I was hurrying through La Morra on my way back to Alba for dinner. In particular, there is a reverence for the dead. A funeral was in progress and a huge old Fiat hearse was parked dramatically in the centre of Piazza Municipio, in front of the church of San Martino, the mourners milling about under the chestnuts, soberly dressed in rustic greys and browns. The service over (most people prefer to participate outside the church, where they can smoke and gossip), the cortège made its slow way through the town, past the Vinbar, to the cemetery, followed at a distance, on foot, by the muffled mourners, praying in unison. The effect, especially in the rain, was chilling.

There are other hill towns, of less interest, in the area, each with its own castle, *trattorie* and particular views. Many of the castles dominating these hill towns originated as watchtowers. Sentries warned the low-lying surrounding districts of the latest and most imminent incursions of the Saracen and Hungarian marauders, who roamed northern Italy in the eighth and ninth centuries in search of booty. The towers were later enlarged, and often formed the feudal base of the district from which one overlord was able to launch an attack on another. Today some are nothing but a pile of ruins, their crenellations overgrown with ivy, while others are private residences or museums. Still others have been turned into restaurants, their banqueting halls converted into dining rooms and their

armouries into storerooms or wine cellars. The original cellars of the castle of Barolo, which started life as a watchtower and later became the residence of the Faletti Marquis of Barolo, now function as the regional *enoteca*. It was, appropriately, in these same cellars that the evolution of the first Barolo wine from the ancient Nebbiolum wine took place. Today Barolo, a rustic village of heavy low brick and stucco houses and muddy alleys, a few kilometres south of La Morra, is of little interest other than that it gave its name to this great wine.

Some of the Langhe towns have quirks which result from their individual gastronomic preoccupations. Until 1960 Roddi d'Alba, between La Morra and Alba, had a university for truffle dogs. Founded in 1880, its first rector, Antonio Moncaliero, was given the name Barot I. It closed down on the death of his successor, Barot II, owing to a lack of competent teaching staff. Mango, to the east of Alba, has a special truffle dog fair in June. Mongrels, *tabui* in the local dialect, are supposed to be the most efficient truffle detectors, and their services are coveted by truffle specialists. At Cherasco are the headquarters for the International Centre and the National Association of Snail Breeders. Both institutions look after the breeding and the commercial aspects of edible snails, and it is not surprising that snails are the town's gastronomic speciality.

Firmly on the gastronomic calendar is Monferrato's October Truffle Fair, held at Moncalvo. Exhibitions of and prize-giving for the best white truffles – valued even more highly for their scent than for their taste – take place here, while at Montiglio a truffle *festa*, also in October, is followed by a tasting session. These October fairs and *feste* are taken extremely seriously, and are the highlight of the year's activities. The truffle season comes at the same time as the grape harvest, the mushrooming season, the game season and the best season

for frogs and snails, but all these ingredients are provided, where possible, throughout the year, by the restaurants, *trattorie* and food shops of the Monferrato towns.

At Moncalvo, the Antico Castello Ristorante, situated at the end of one of the two arcades in Piazza Garibaldi, in one of the few remaining rooms of its medieval castle, provides fairly basic, simple cooking. The Via xx Settembre, which runs from the bottom of the town to the Piazza Garibaldi at the top, is thick with vegetable shops and butchers. The Piemontese eat a lot of red meat, the rédder the better. In fact, raw beef thinly sliced – *carne cruda* – and dressed simply with oil and vinegar is a fairly popular dish. The *pasticceria* at number 5 Piazza Garibaldi has *torta alle nocciole*, a light but rich, buttery hazelnut cake, while Pastificio Gastronomia Rondaco, in the Via xx Settembre, sells *ravioli* stuffed with truffles.

Two hill towns in Piedmont: La Morra (above) and Serralunga d'Alba at dusk (overleaf).

INDEX

ACKNOWLEDGMENTS

Greatest thanks to Paola Greco of the Italian Tourist Office in London, and to Anne Engel.

Many thanks also to Gigliola Lantini of the ENIT in Rome and to the representatives of the Departments of Tourism in the various regional governments, in particular those of Basilicata, Calabria, Apulia, Tuscany, Liguria, Piedmont, Val D'Aosta, Trentino and Sardinia.

Special thanks, for their help, advice and encouragement, to Remy Blumenfeld, Lucinda Bredin, Juliet and Will Camp, Camilla and Giorgio Canovi, the Doria Pamphilj family, Carlo Ducci, Iris Jones (Archivio Doria Pamphilj), Willie Landels, Luca Leoncini, Guy and Betsy de Lotbinière, Carolyn Quartermaine, Caroline Robertson, Conrad Roeber, Johnnie Shand Kydd and Judith Watt.

Thanks also to Maggiore Autonoleggio, one of whose cars I drove over a precipice in a rainstorm.

The publishers wish to thank Ghigo Roli for supplying the photographs on pages 75, 76 and 77.